How to Draw
NeoPopRealism
abstract IMAGES

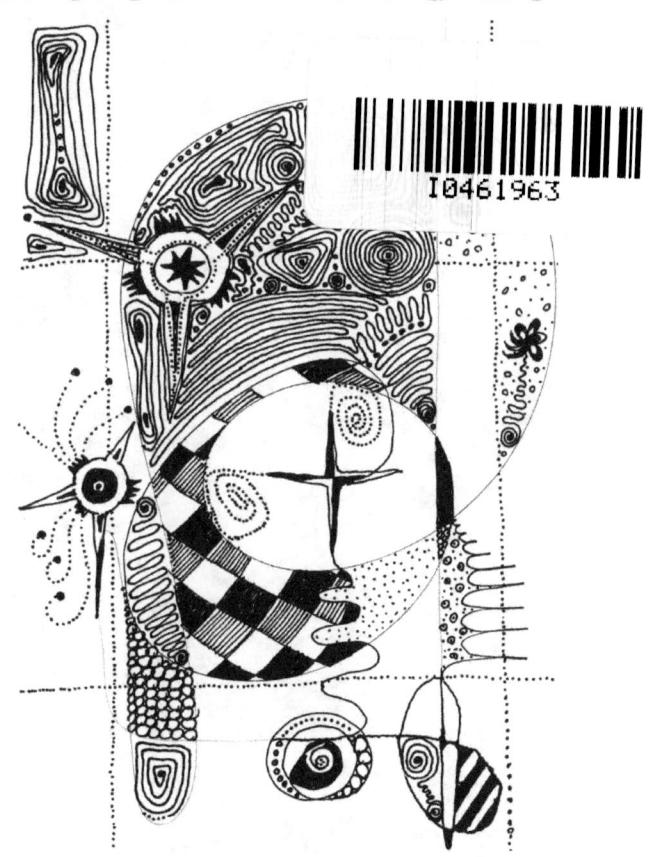

Ink Backgrounds

NeoPopRealism PRESS
ILLUSTRATED BY NADIA RUSS

I0461963

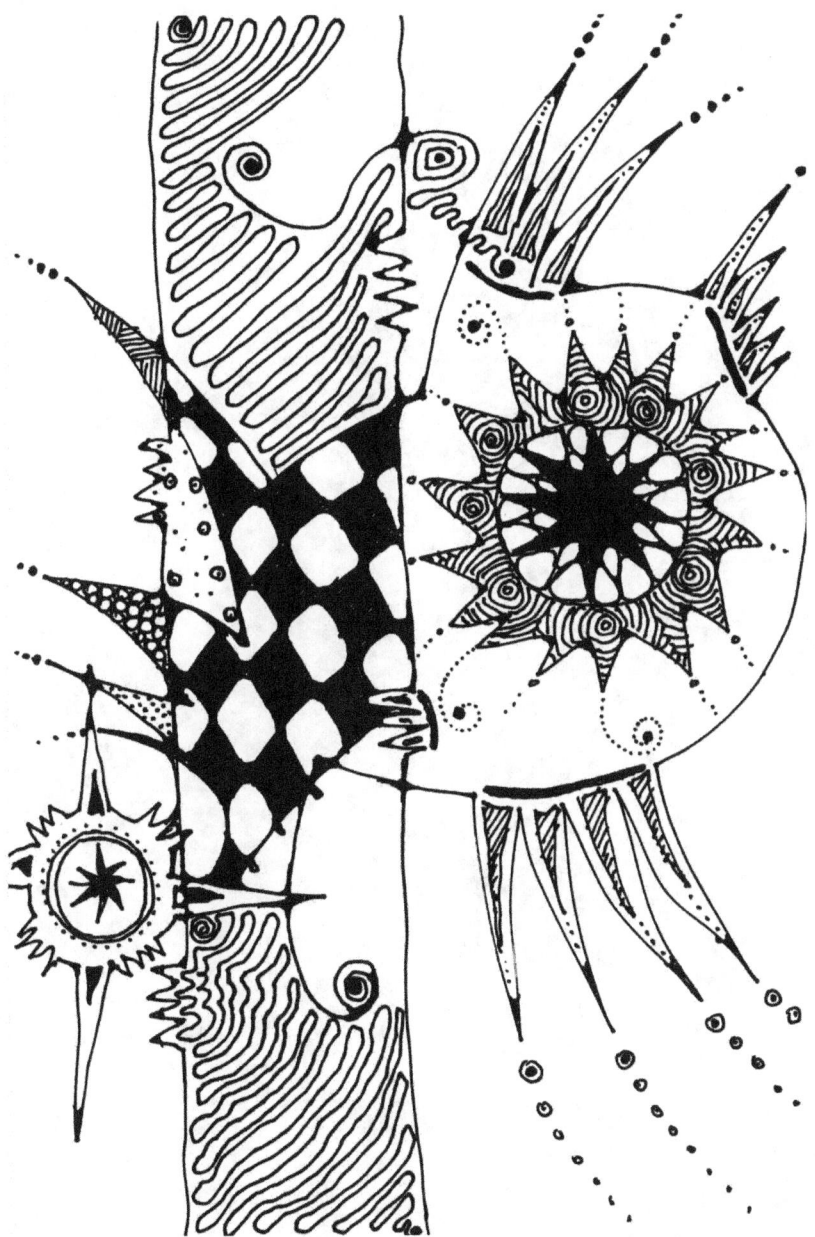

Nadia Russ, Abstract 1, *Meditation 11*, Ink on paper

NeoPopRealist artworks' backgrounds are whimsical. They are simple and complicated at the same time as any abstract.

4

How to Draw
NeoPopRealism
abstract IMAGES

Ink Backgrounds

NeoPopRealism PRESS
ILLUSTRATED BY **NADIA RUSS**

First time published in 2011 by NeoPopRealism PRESS
PO BOX 366
New York, NY 10013

NeoPopRealismPRESS@mail.com

How to Draw NeoPopRealism Abstract: Ink Backgrounds

© Copyrighted in 2011 by NeoPopRealism PRESS and Nadia Russ

All rights reserved. Apart from any fair dealing for the purpose of the criticism, review, or personal study of the reader, no part of this book may be reproduced, stored in a retrieval system, or transmitted in any form or by any means, electronic or mechanical, including photocopy, without the prior written permission of the copyright owner. Enquires should be addressed to the Publisher.
Neither Authors nor Publisher can be responsible for any losses, injuries, and other damages which may result from the use of the information in this book.

ISBN-13: 978-0615527437
ISBN-10: 0615527434

11 12 13 14 15   10 9 8 7 6 5 4 3 2 1

Published in the United States of America
Language: English

This book teaches how to draw NeoPopRealism abstracts / ink backgrounds.

For teenagers and adults

Author: NeoPopRealism PRESS
Illustrated by Nadia Russ

www.neopoprealism.org

CONTENT

1. Content ....…….. 7
2. Introduction ....….. 8
3. Get inspired ....…. 9
4. How to create a simplified NeoPopRealist abstract 11
5. How to create advanced NeoPopRealist abstract 22
6. Create abstracts with Nadia Russ 33
7. Create your repetitive patterns gallery 55
8. Create your abstract drawings from the scratch....... 60
9. About NeoPopRealism creator Nadia Russ 73
10. Conclusion 74

INTRODUCTION

NeoPopRealism ink drawing concept was created by Nadia Russ in 1989. It was an experiment. She was trying to connect to the Universe and let the Universe use her as a Conductor when she created her drawings. She didn't want to follow any other artists' achievements, she decided to create absolutely new art form, like Picasso (Cubism), Dali (Surrealism), Andy Warhol (Pop Art) and a few other worldwide known artists had done.

Nadia Russ took her ink pen and began to draw a flowing line that turned into shapes, figures, often faces. Then, some sections (or all), that appeared, she filled with the repetitive patterns. She never uses eraser because if a mistake made, it disappears with the following repetitive patterns that balance the whole composition. Her work was unique; no one did anything like this before.

Later, January 4, 2003, Nadia Russ created a word NeoPopRealism and internationally announced new style of visual arts.

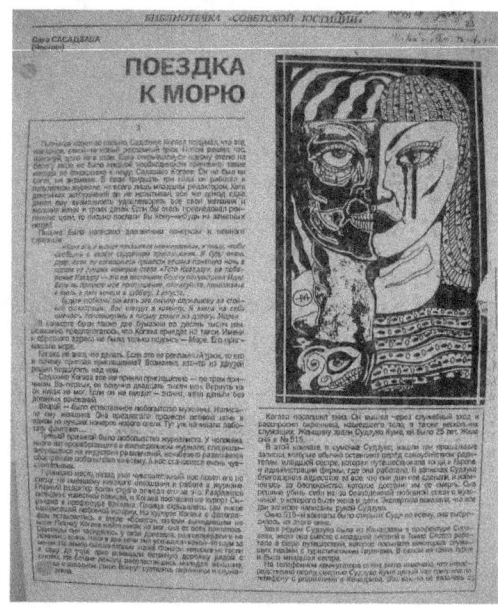

Nadia Russ illustrated a story by Saho Sasadzava for the *Russian Justice* Journal, 1992, Moscow, Russia

Get inspired

When you focus on success, you fall into the trap of comparing yourself to others, feeling envious. Instead, focus on getting better every day, focus on excellence. Gratitude floods your body and brain with emotions that uplift and energize you. Use your strengths for a bigger purpose beyond yourself. Focus on what you are giving instead of what you are getting, it makes every your step more rewarding and meaningful. . .

Your artwork is reflection of you, your moods; also it depends on what your artistic task is. Some of your NeoPopRealism work can have light backgrounds, but other - very busy, with the complicated-looking, whimsical ornaments, where line twists and turns seemed unpredictably. The drawing of the busy abstracts/backgrounds is meditative process. The meditative state of mind is the highest state in which the mind exists. When you are drawing your whimsical ornaments, your mind is open for the renewal. And more you draw, more relaxed you are. The repetitive patterns' drawing process invites you to the world where everything is simple as the sun and sky, and you are mesmerized by this simplicity and by the drawing process itself.

After you finish one pattern, you begin draw anther, and so on. The images look complicated, but not all are that complicated when you start execute them. Concept is: *Line creates sections; sections fill with the repetitive patterns, using ink pen. You never use eraser.* With this drawing method you can achieve not only the interesting artistic results, but also the purity of your mind. Use your imagination. It is like a journey to the world of unknown with good feeling, knowing that you can turn the complexity into simplicity. This drawing is intuitive. Believe in yourself: you are a magician who can execute magic with the ink pen. You need no eraser because if a 'mistake' happened, it disappears with the following repetitive patterns that balance the whole composition. Isn't that magic?

Get your black ink pen *Foray Rolle Rollerball Medium 0.7 mm, Sharpie* or any similar and a piece of cardstock paper 8.5"x11". Cut paper into two pieces, 5.5"x8.5" each. Now, you need one piece. In future, you can use ink pen - thin or thick - and type and size of paper depending on your artistic tasks.

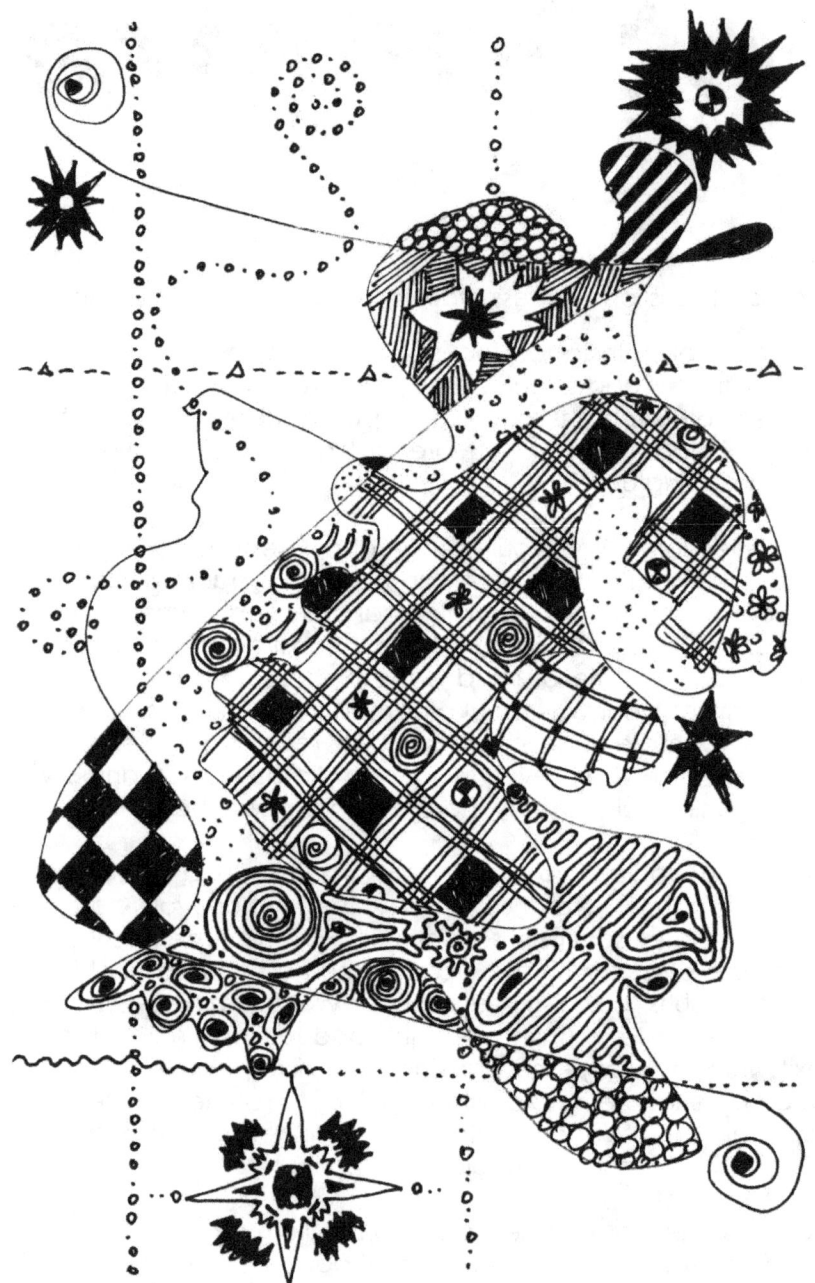

Nadia Russ, Abstract 2, *Meditation 12*, ink on paper

How to create a simplified NeoPopRealist abstract

The following pages will show you step-by-step how to create a simplified abstract background for NeoPopRealism ink artwork that contains faces, figures or other objects. Also you can use such abstract as the independent graphic design. You need no special skills to draw this abstract. If you can draw line, circles, triangles, squares and ovals, you will be able to create this kind of NeoPopRealism abstract ink drawings. Every following picture includes new details. The complete image looks like this:

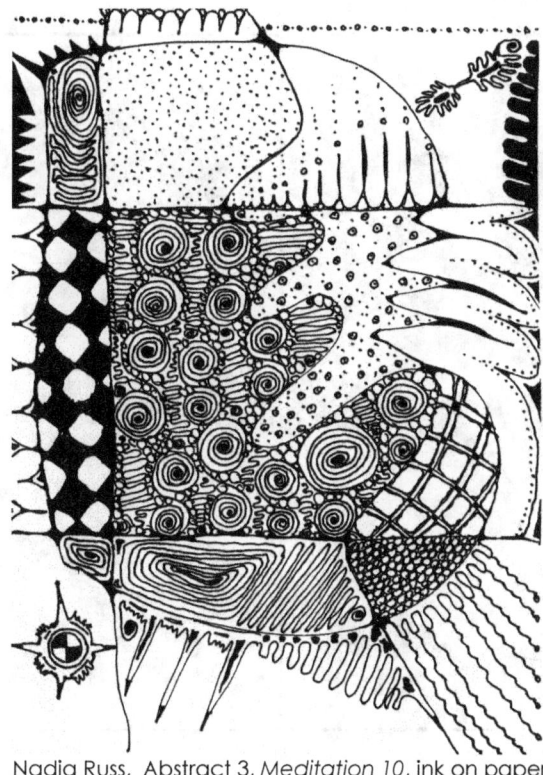

Nadia Russ, Abstract 3, *Meditation 10*, ink on paper

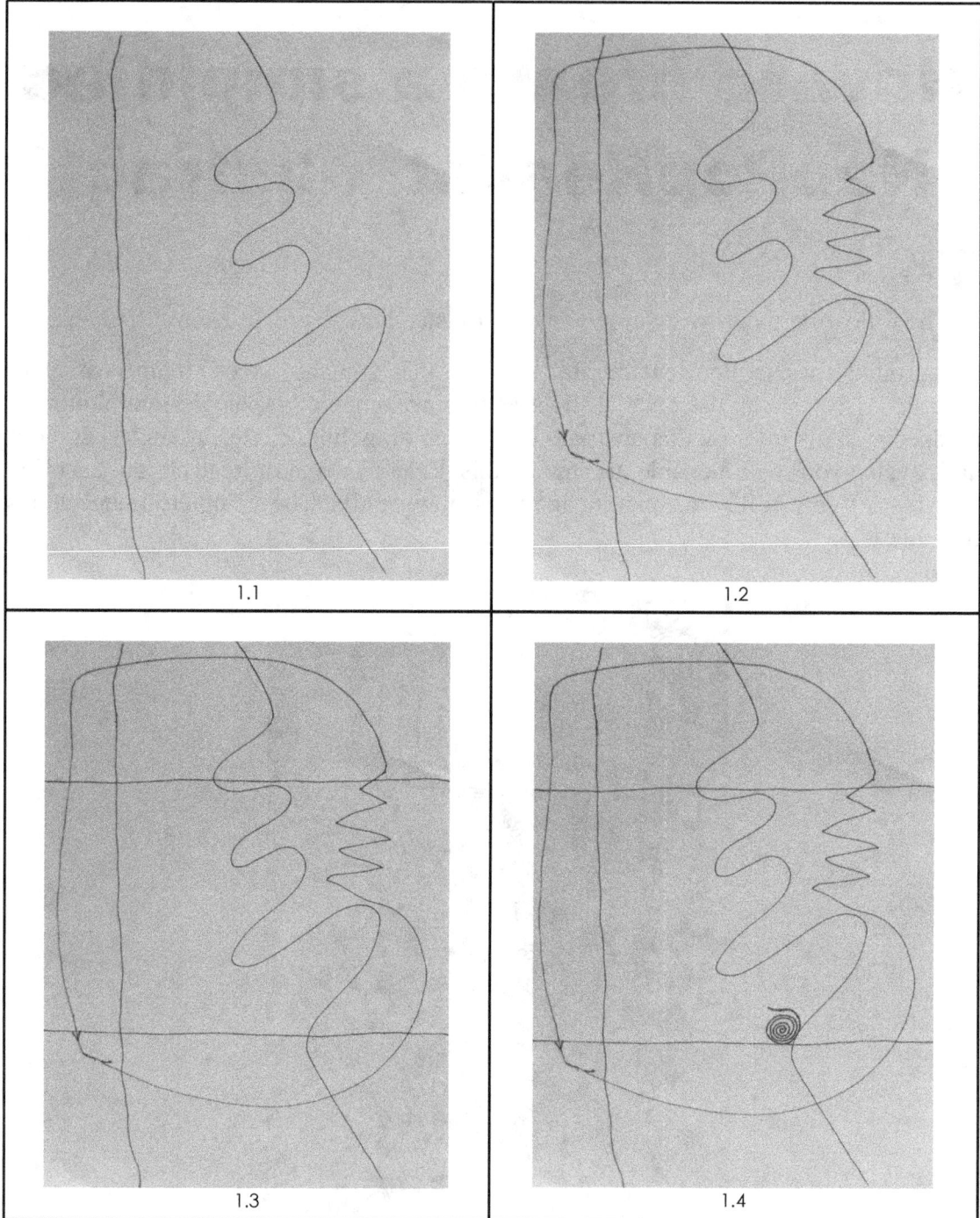

1.1

1.2

1.3

1.4

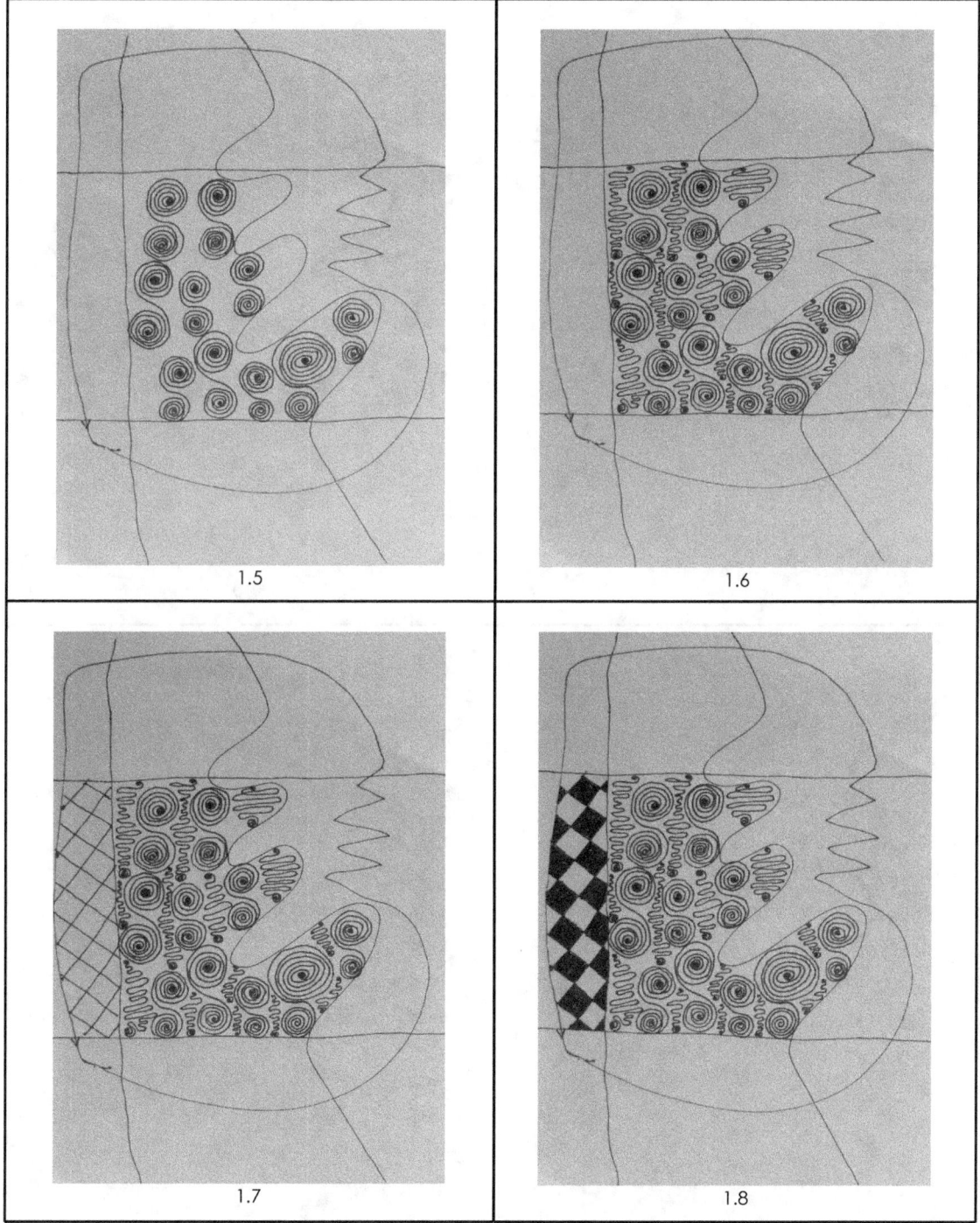

1.5

1.6

1.7

1.8

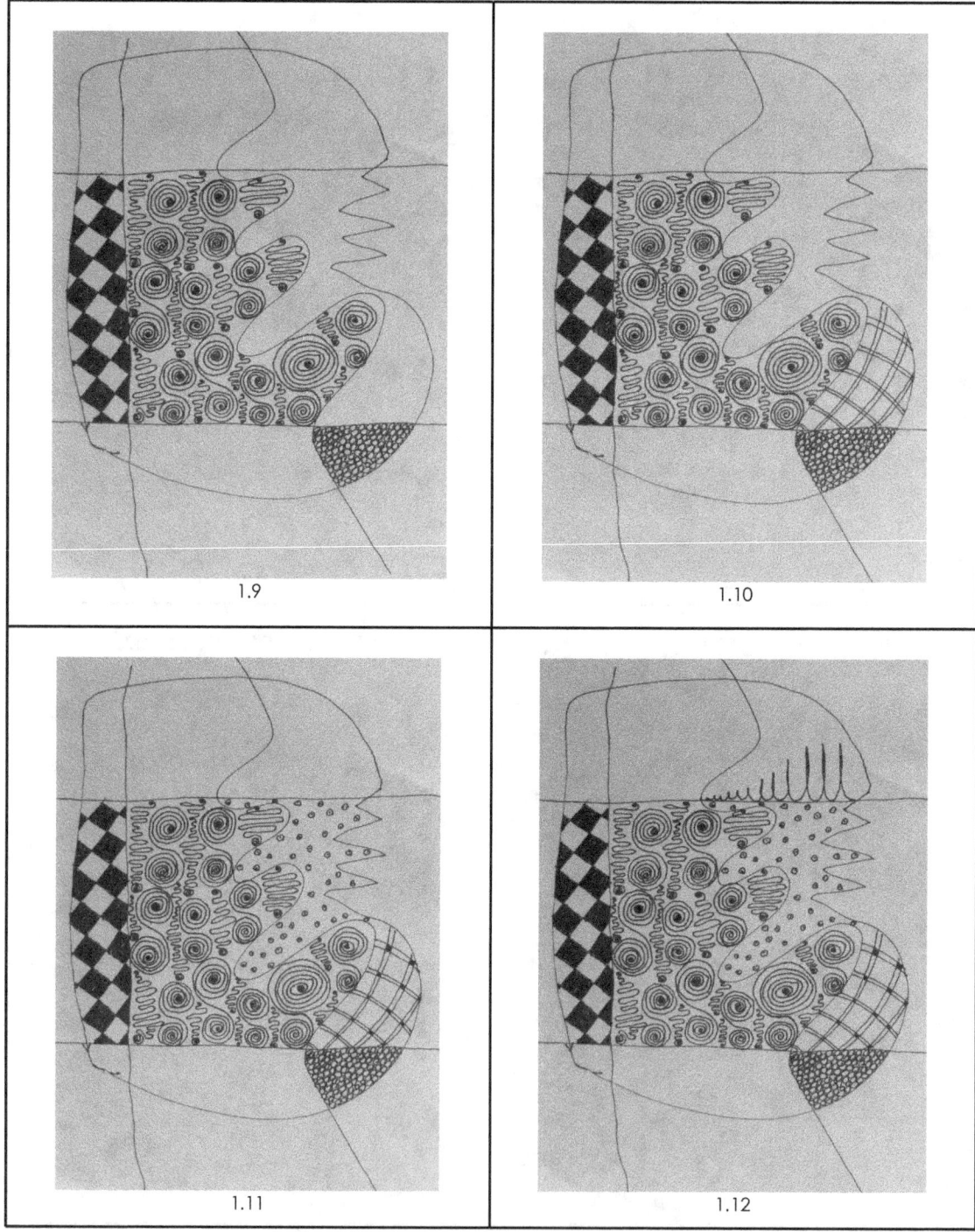

1.9

1.10

1.11

1.12

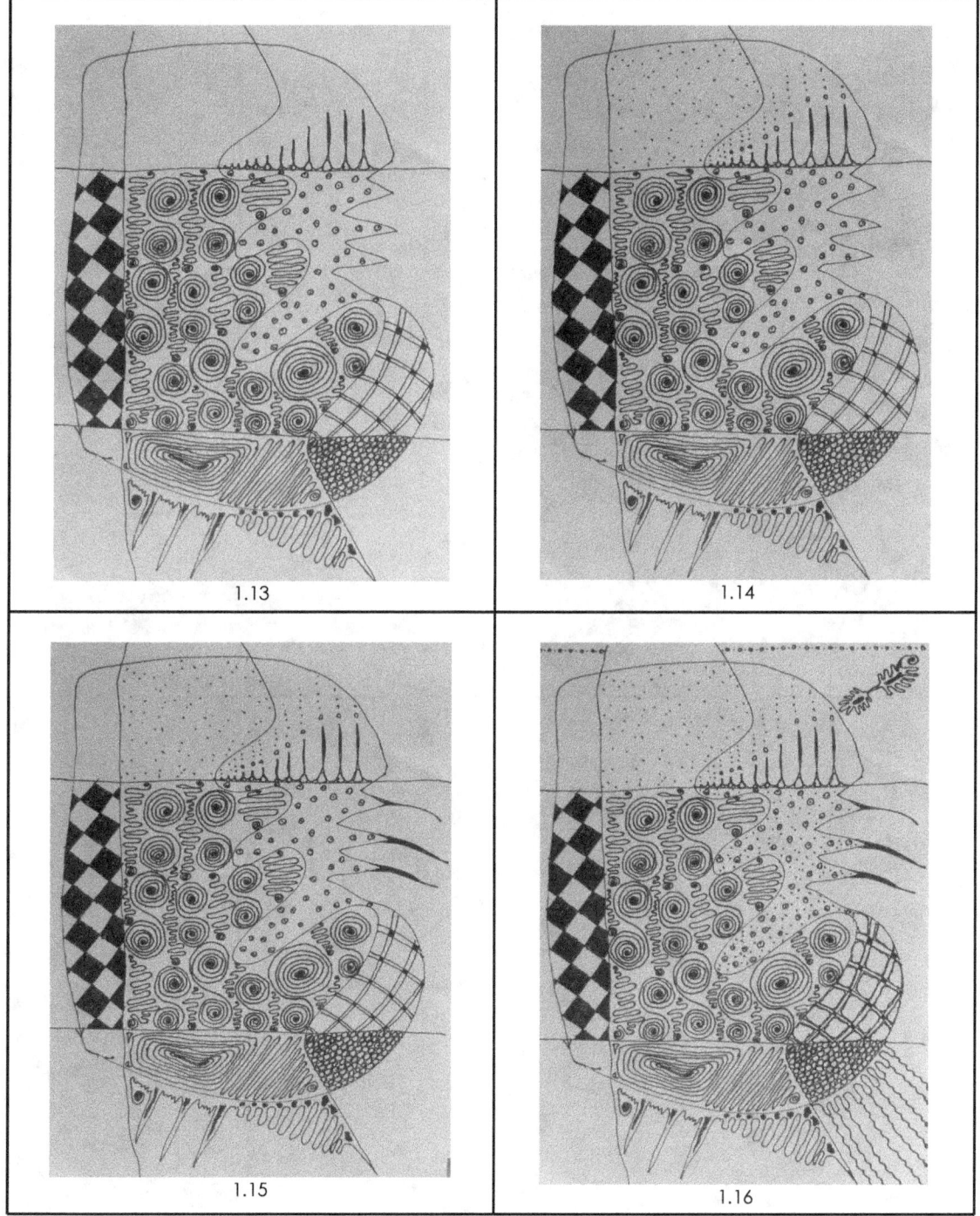

1.13

1.14

1.15

1.16

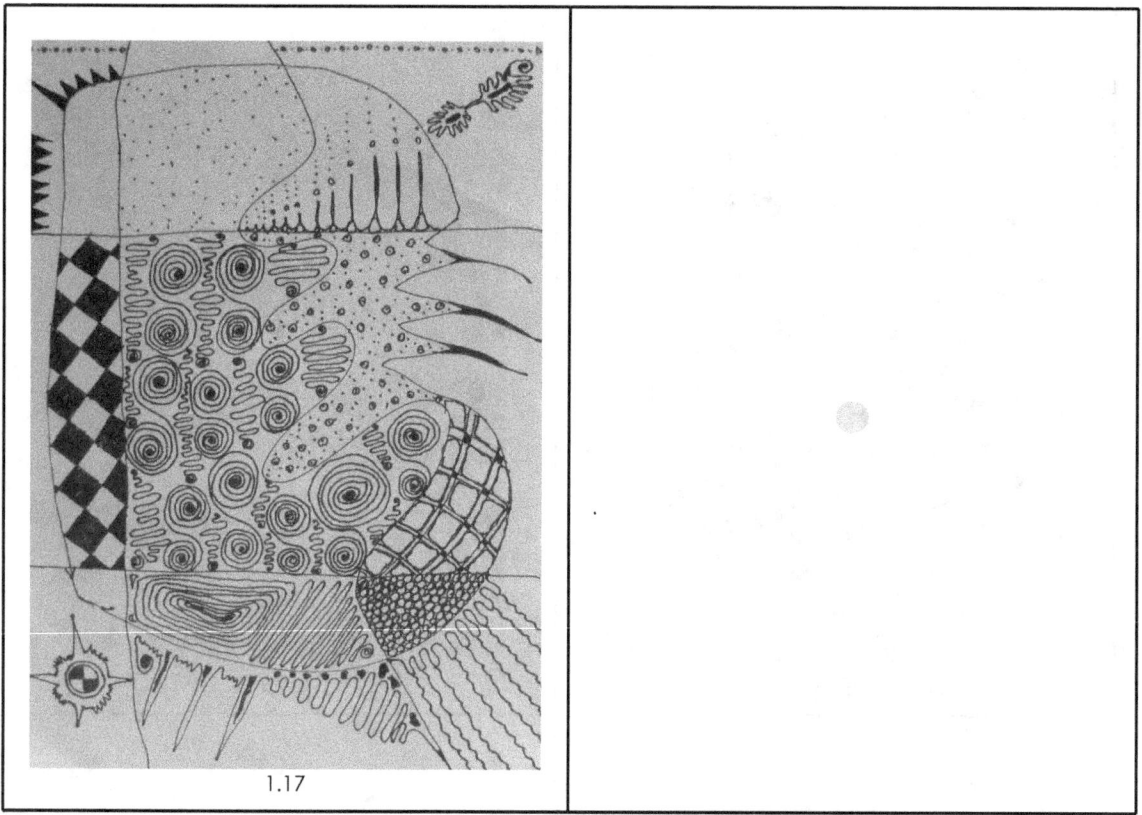

1.17

The following pages (17-21) will show you how to draw repetitive patterns, used in NeoPopRealism ink Abstract 3. Every next image of each pattern includes new detail. Now you see that the complicated looking drawing made with simple patterns.

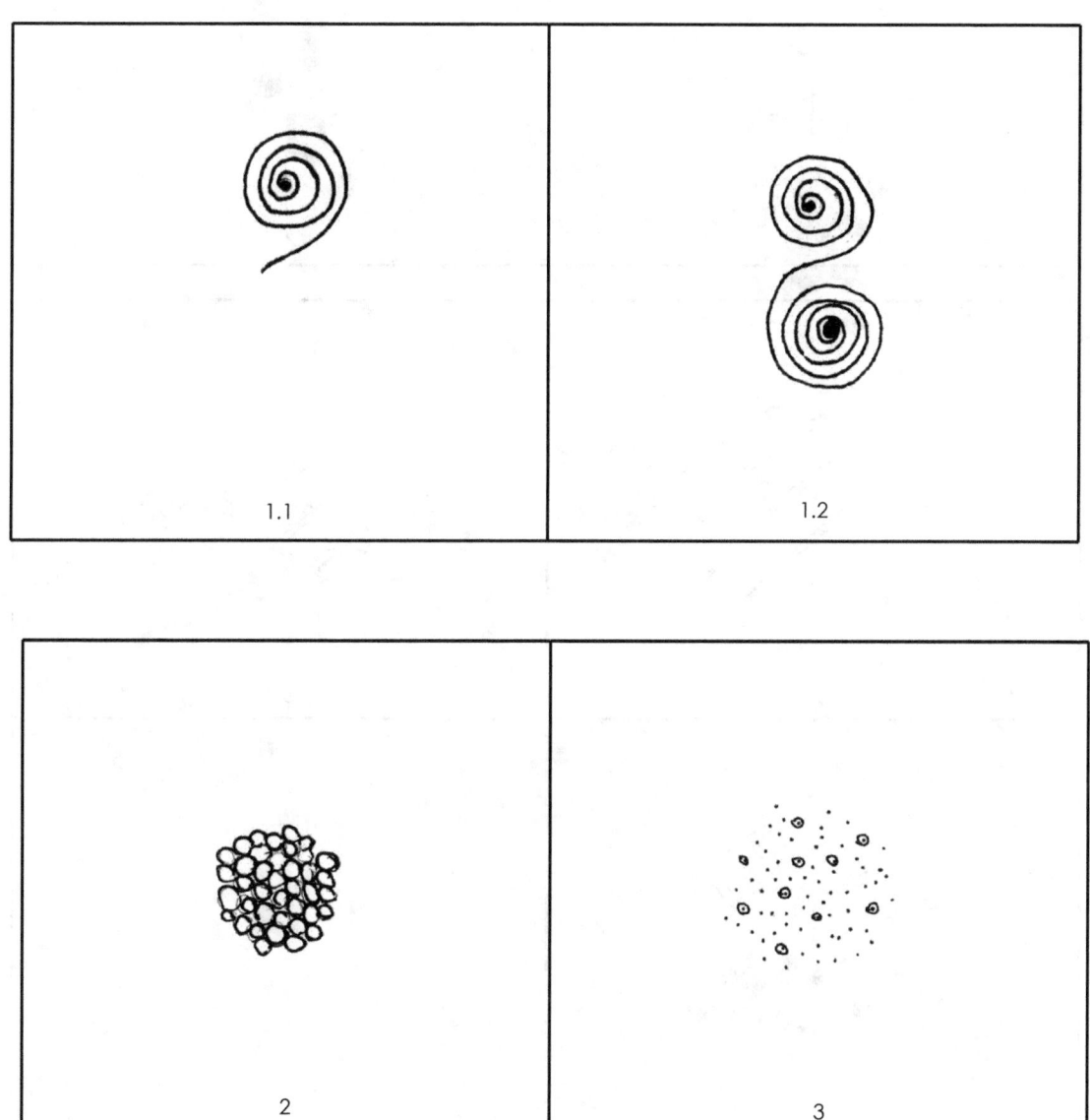

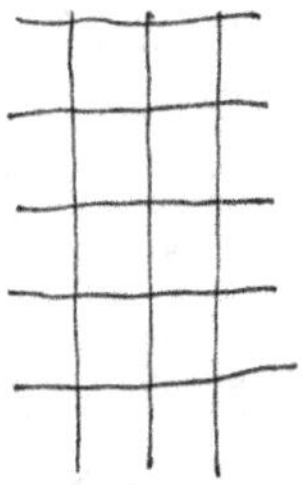

4.1

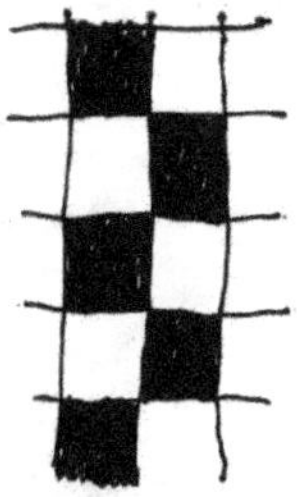

4.2

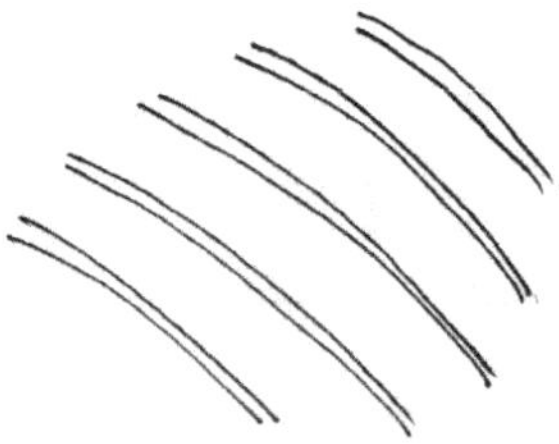

5.1

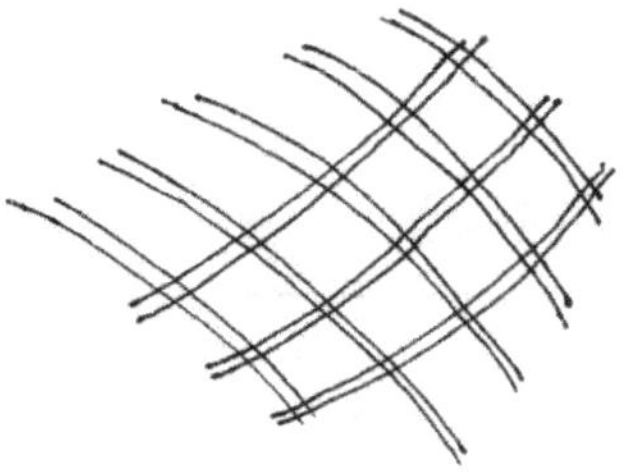

5.2

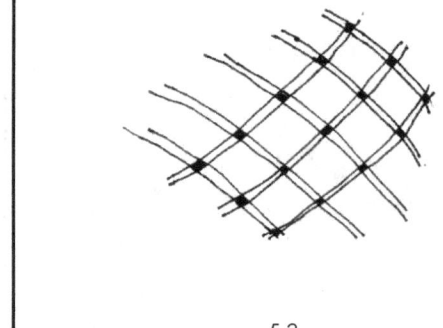

5.3

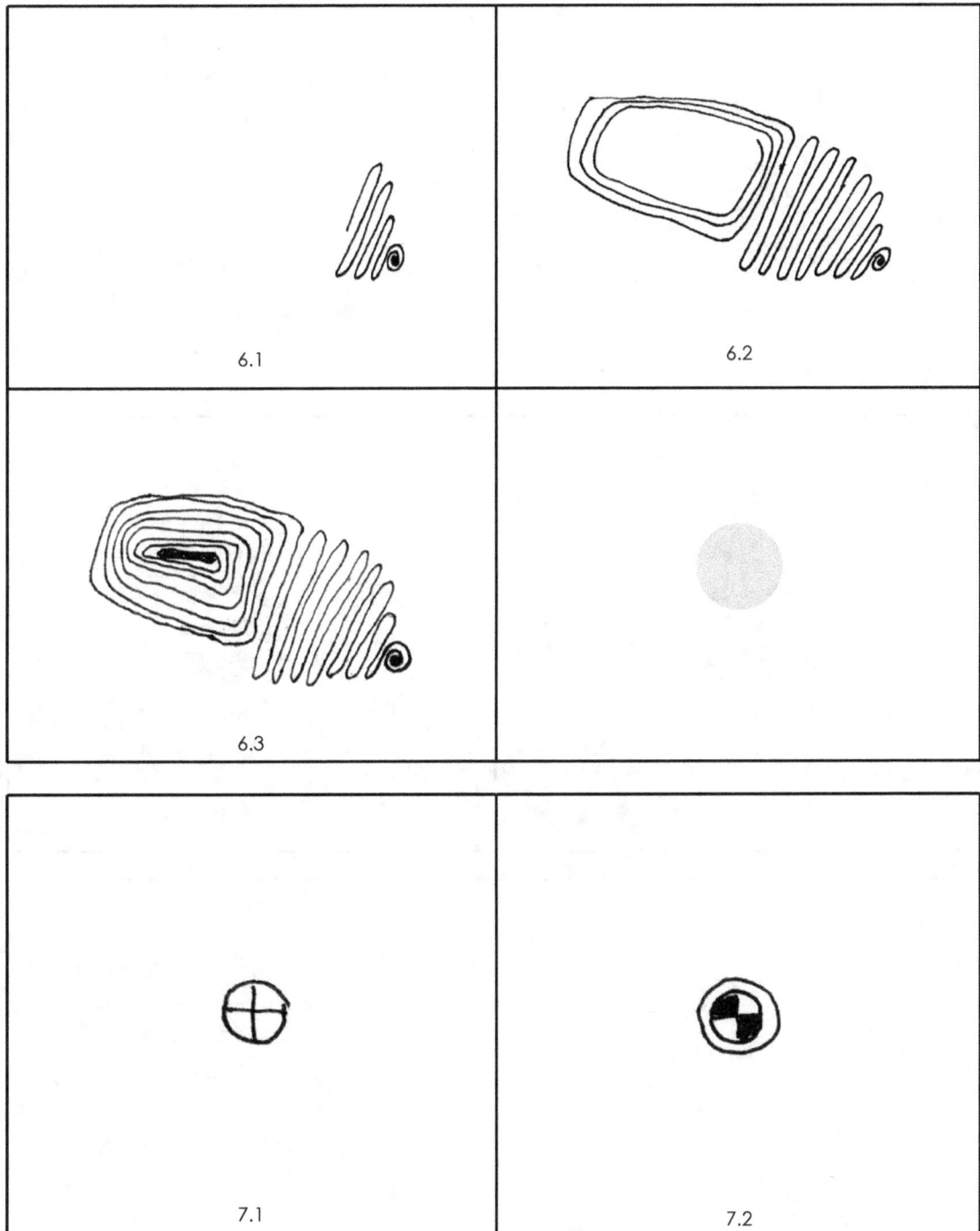

6.1

6.2

6.3

7.1

7.2

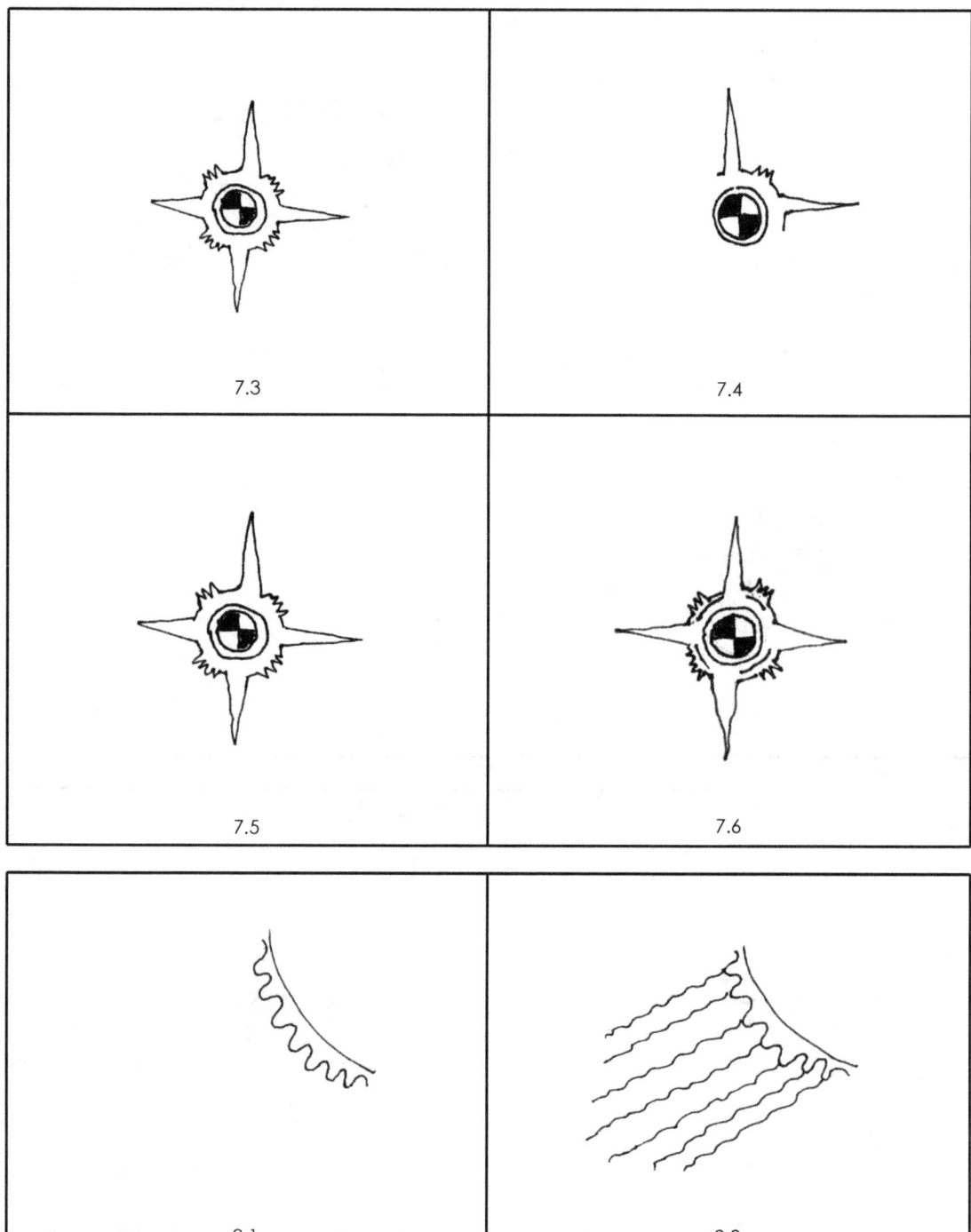

7.3

7.4

7.5

7.6

8.1

8.2

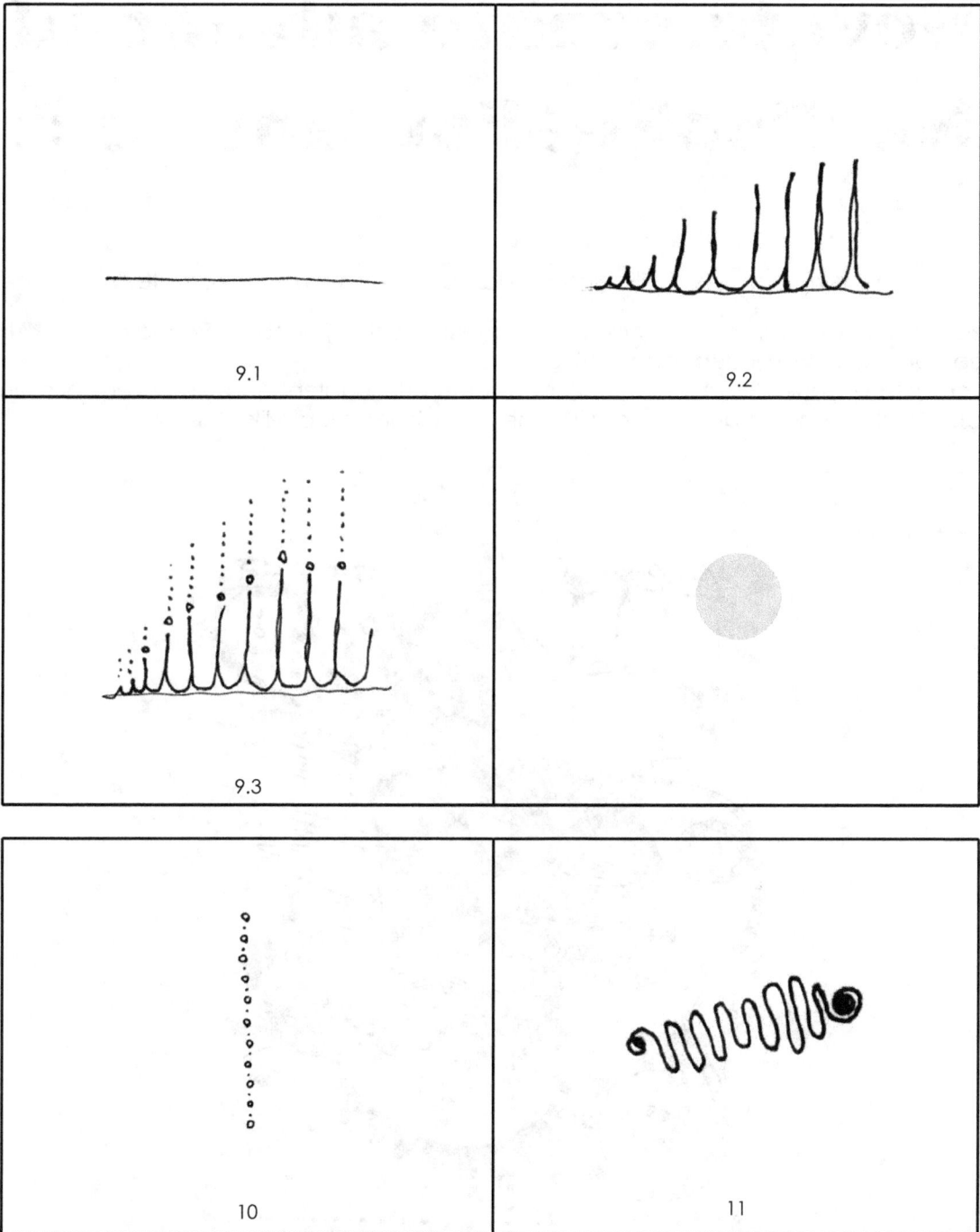

9.1

9.2

9.3

10

11

How to create advanced NeoPopRealist abstract

The following pages will show step-by-step how to create advanced NeoPopRealism abstracts that can be used as the backgrounds in your drawings. Also it can be used as an independent ink design.

To create this particular abstract you need some artistic talent and skills. Every following picture includes new additional details; the final abstract looks like this:

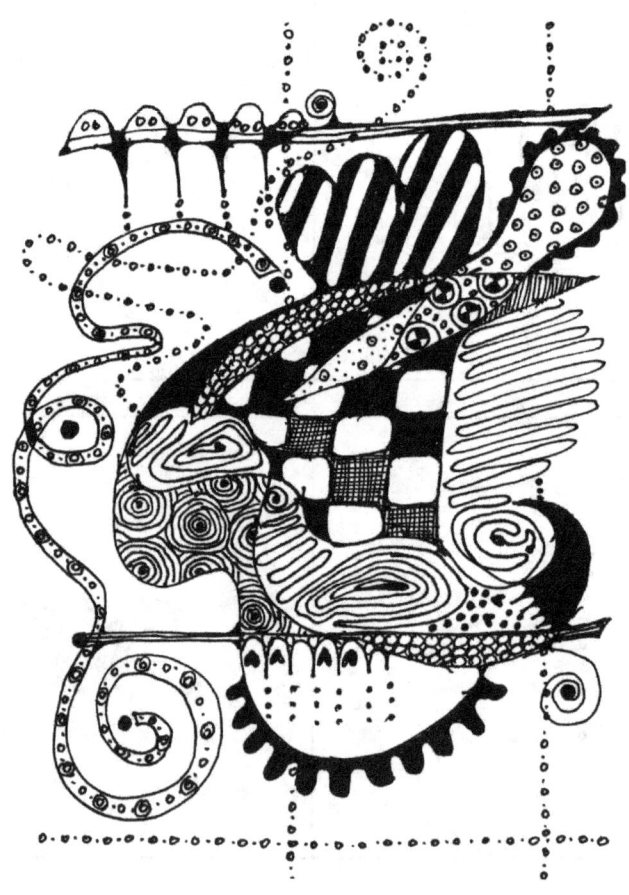

Nadia Russ, Abstract 4, *Meditation 9* , ink on paper

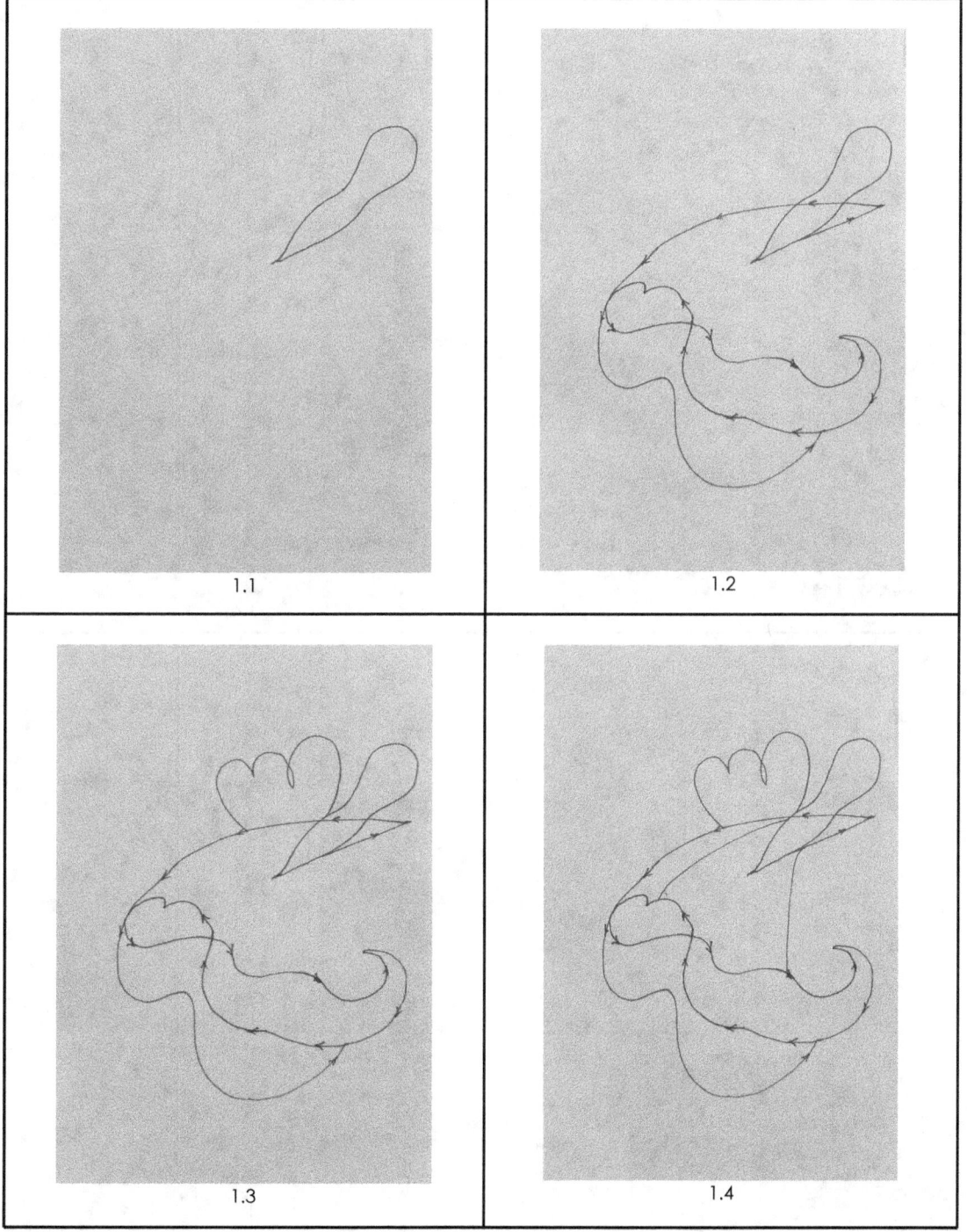

1.1

1.2

1.3

1.4

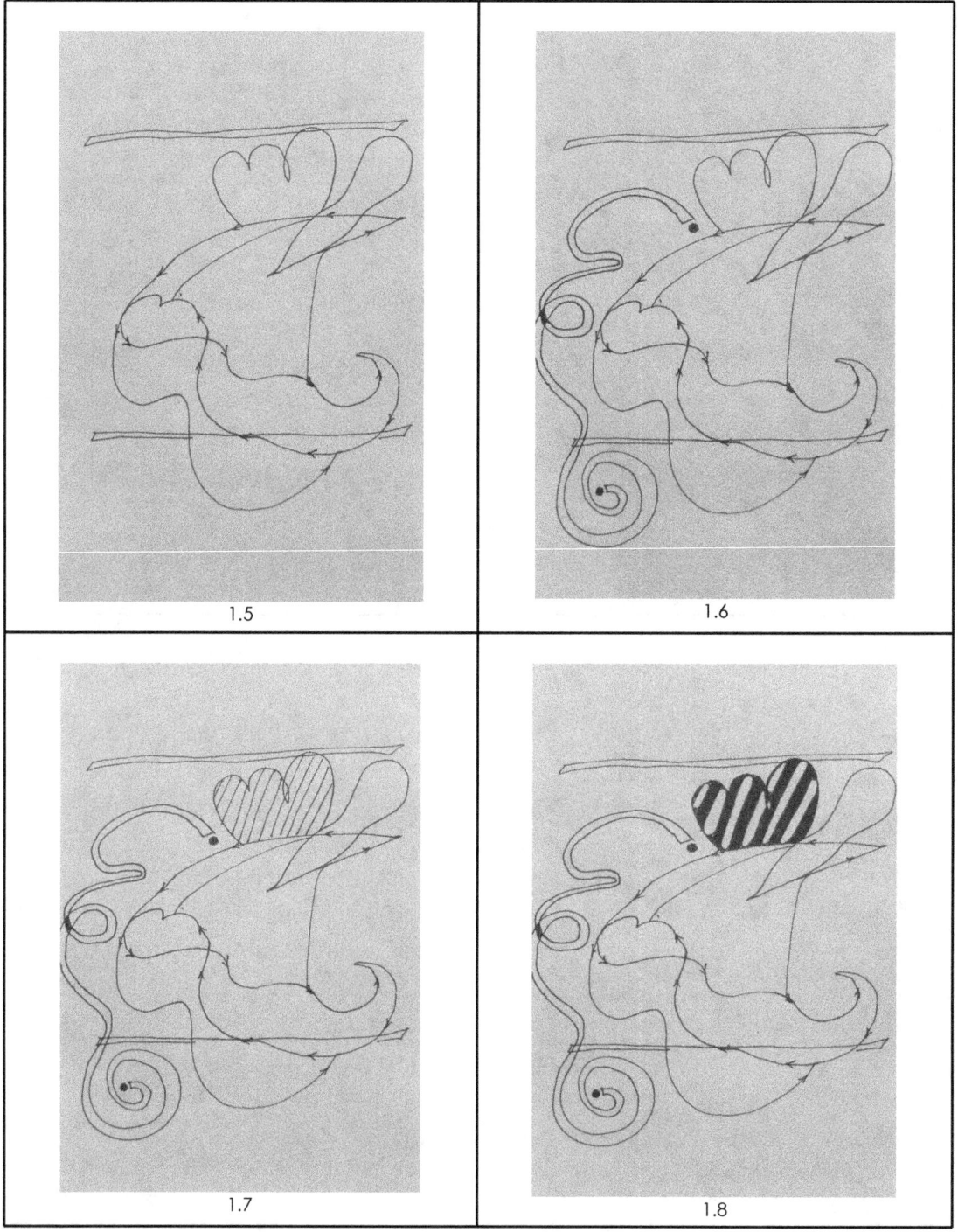

1.5

1.6

1.7

1.8

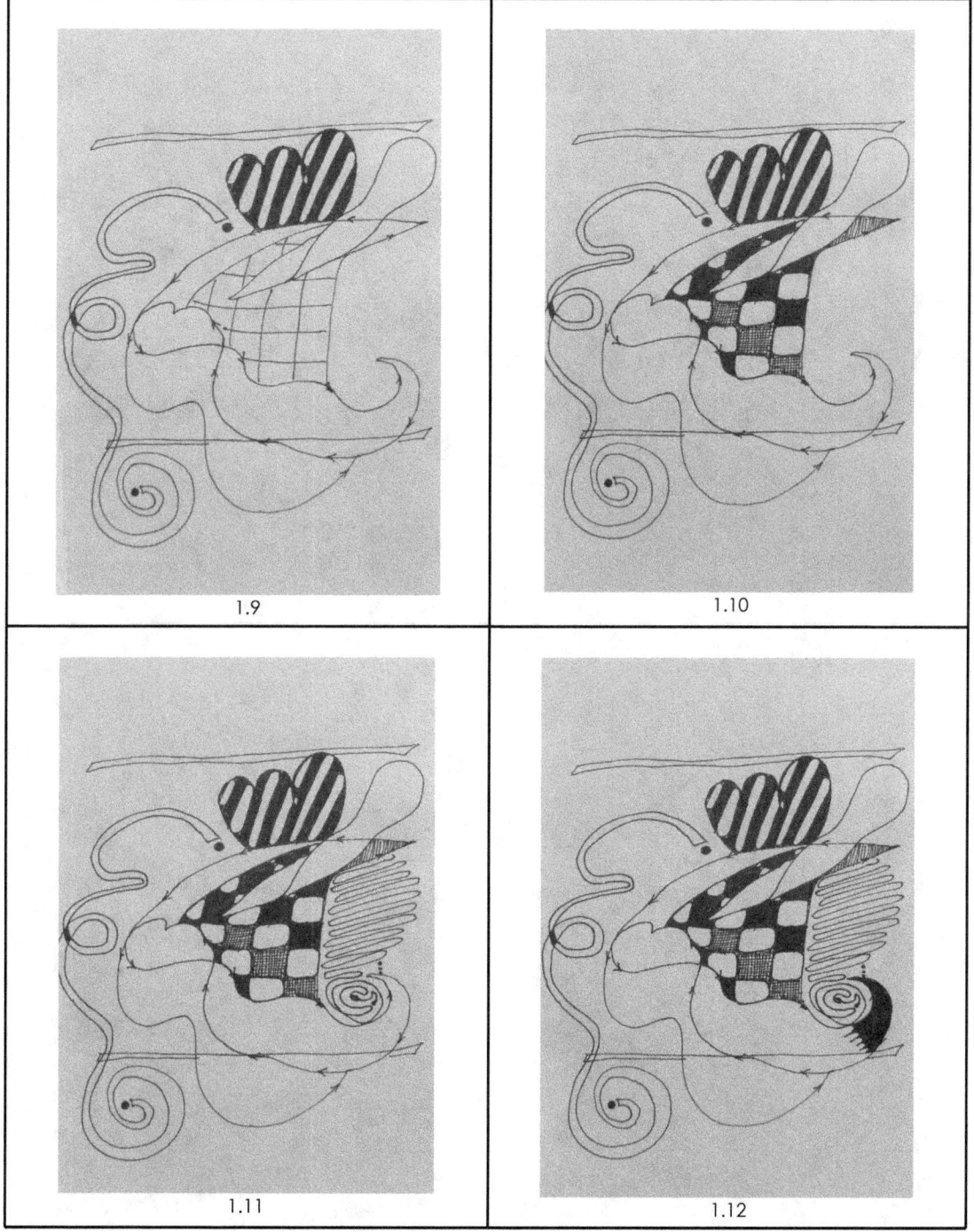

1.9

1.10

1.11

1.12

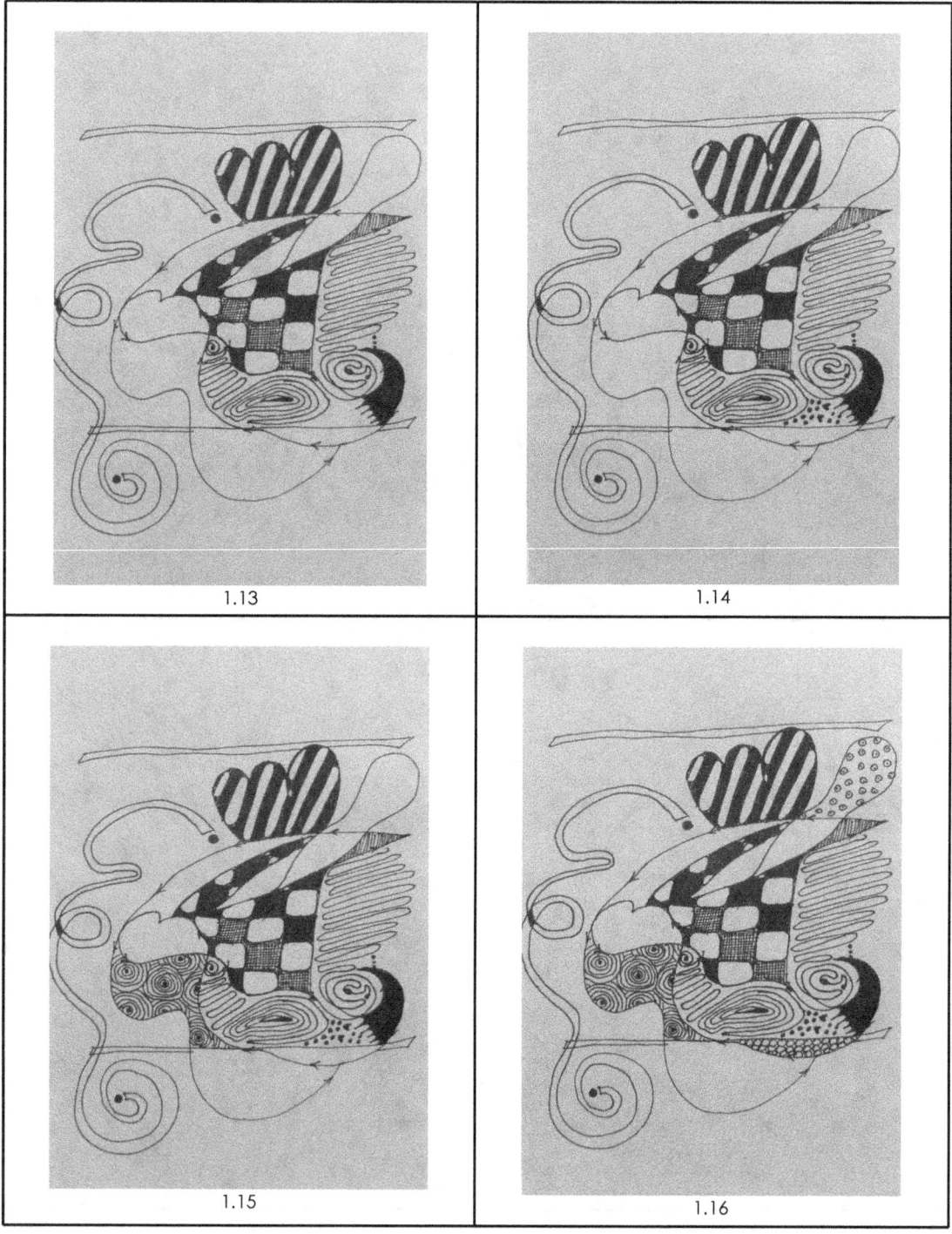

1.13

1.14

1.15

1.16

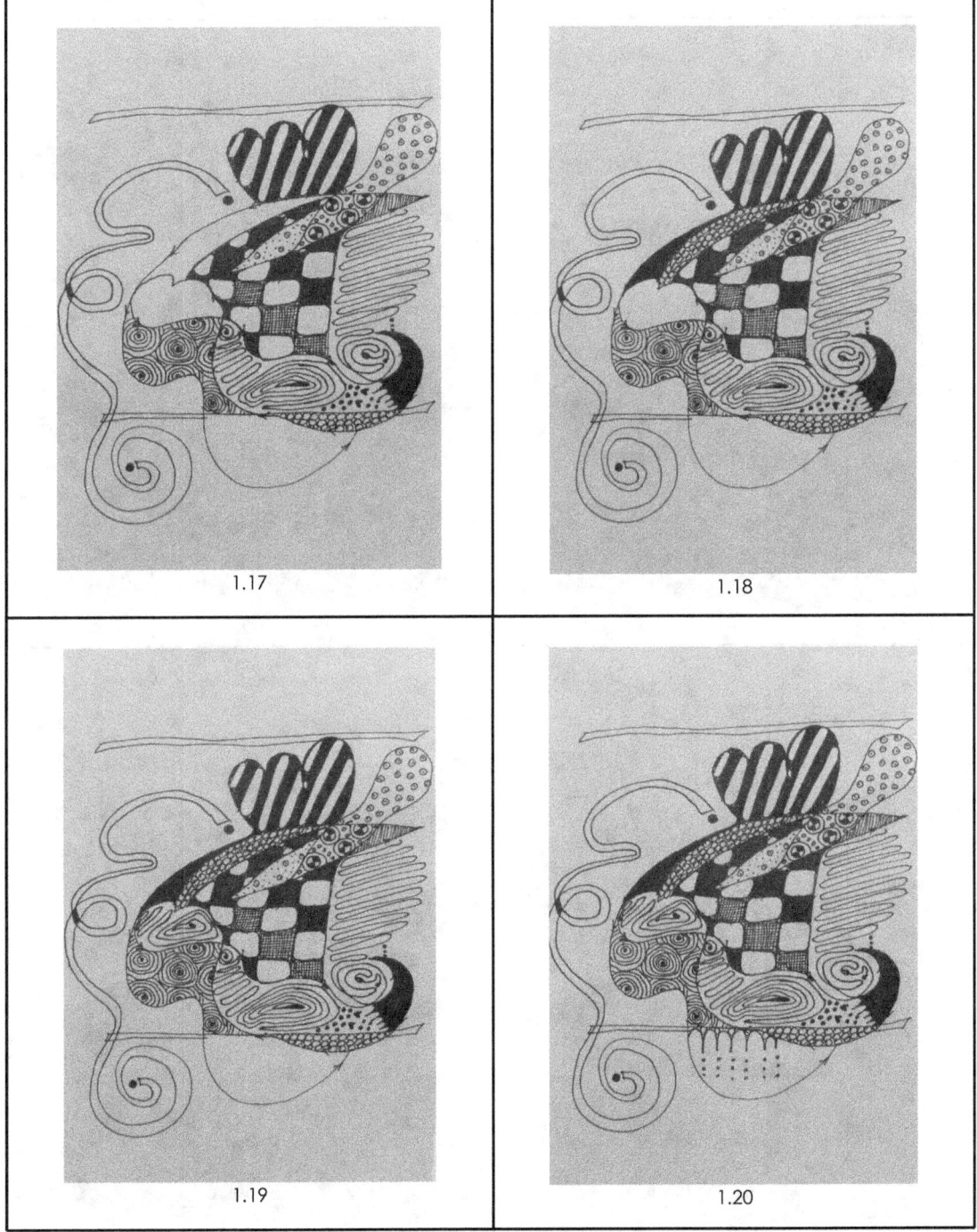

1.17

1.18

1.19

1.20

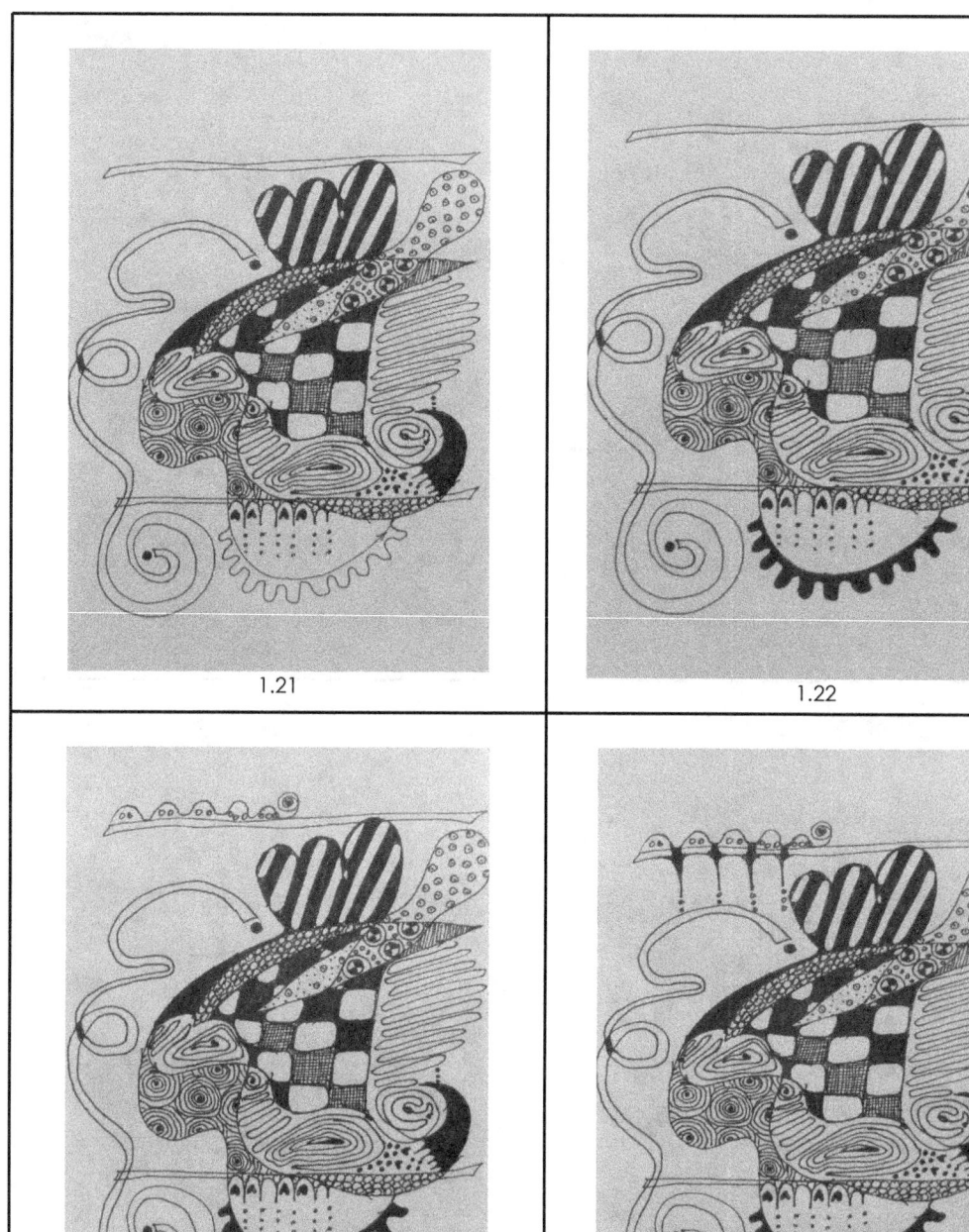

1.21

1.22

1.23

1.24

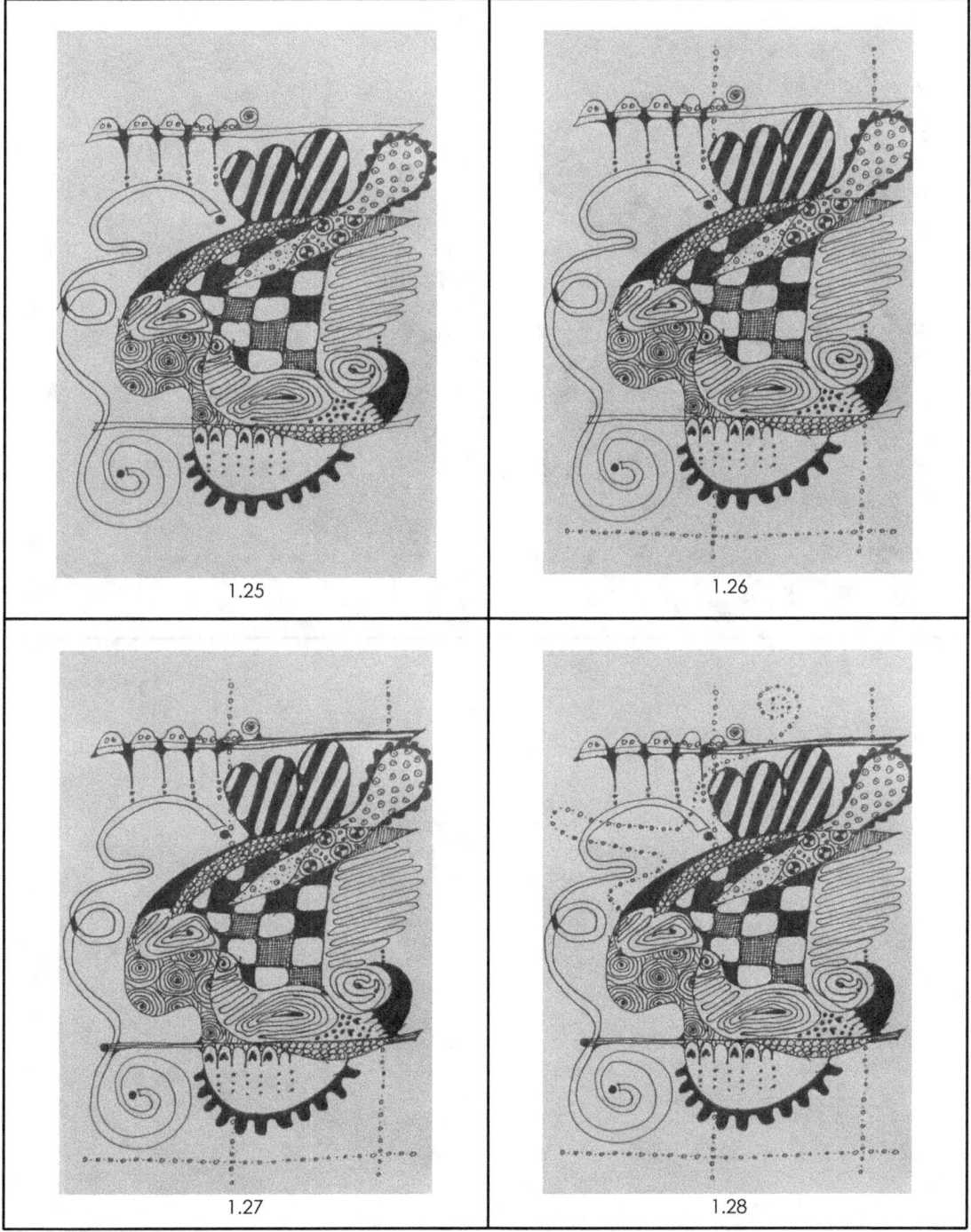

1.25

1.26

1.27

1.28

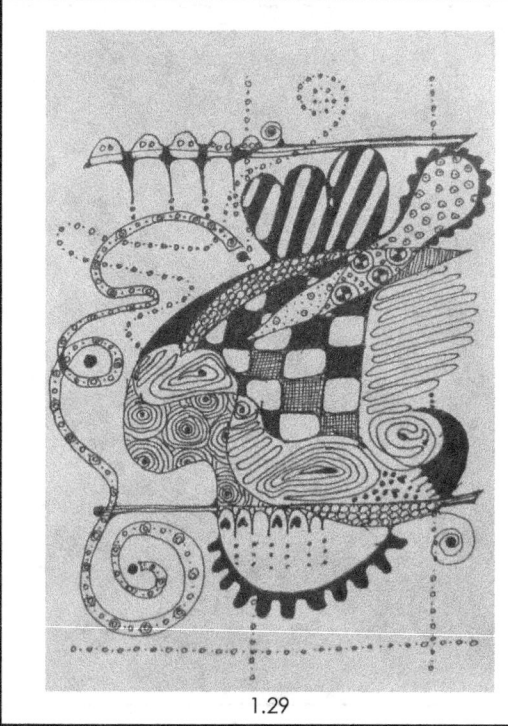

1.29

Visual instructions on how to draw repetitive patterns, used in this abstract, you will find in pages 17-21 and 29-31.

The following pages will show you how to draw the repetitive patterns, used in NeoPopRealism ink Abstract 4. Every next image of each pattern includes new detail(s).

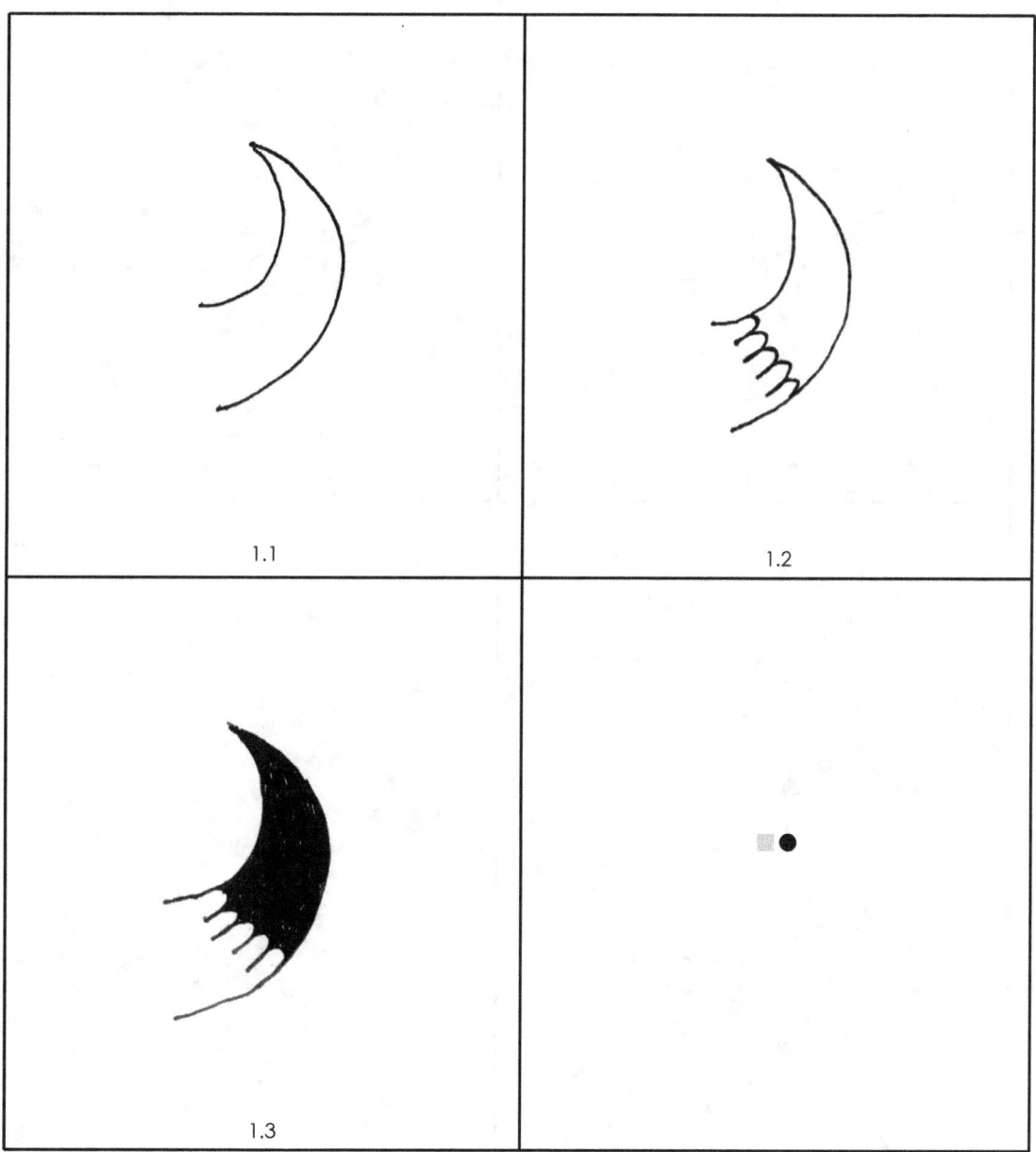

1.1

1.2

1.3

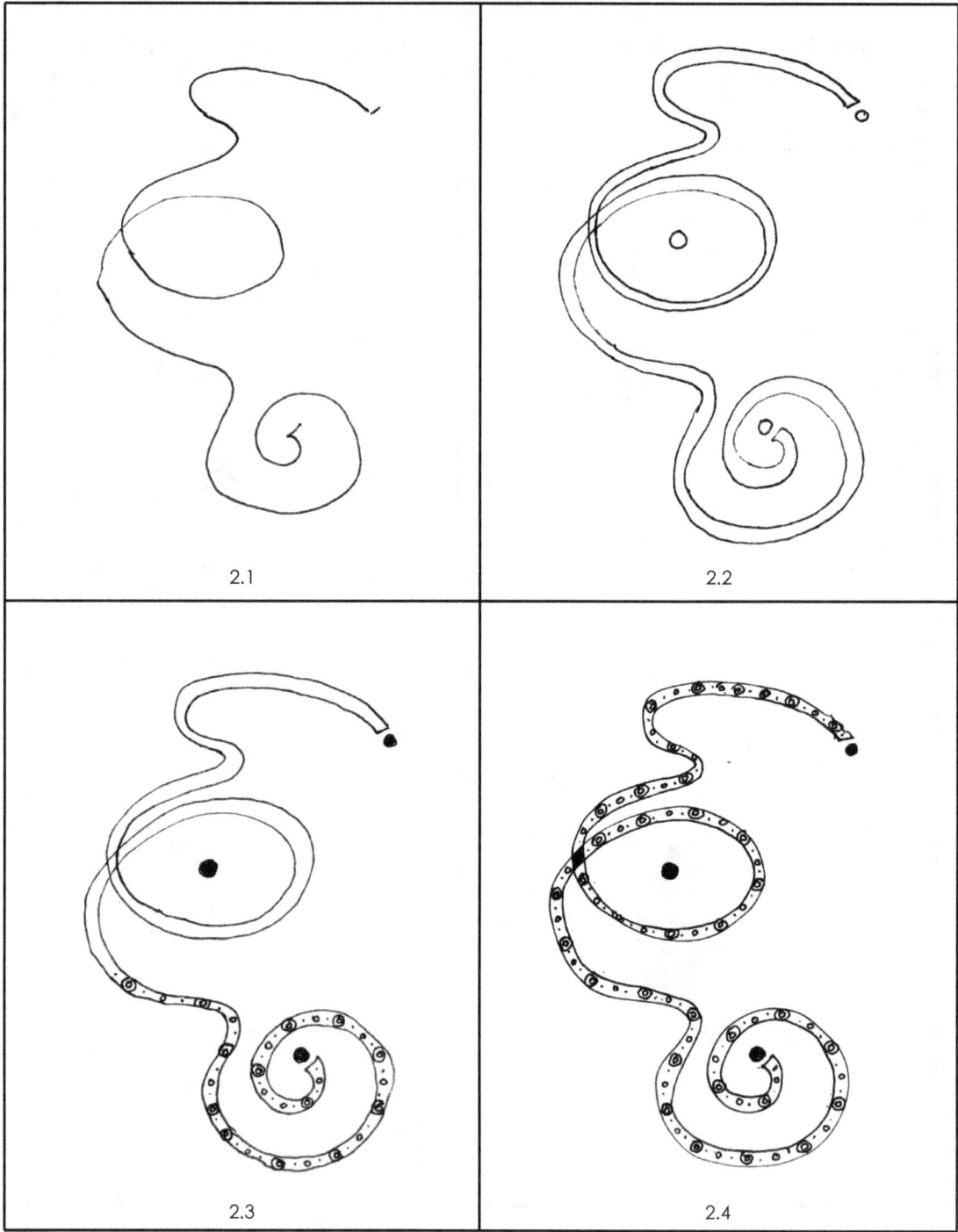

2.1

2.2

2.3

2.4

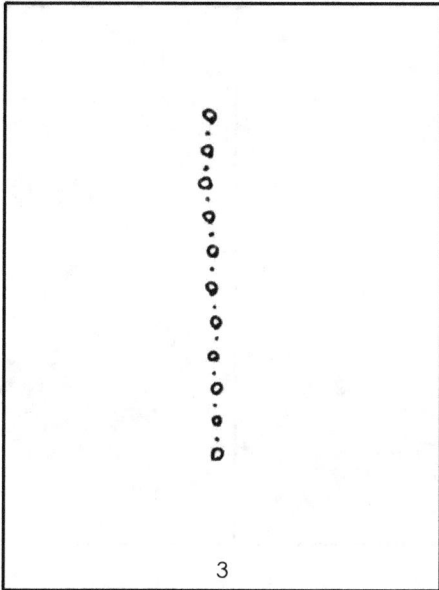

3

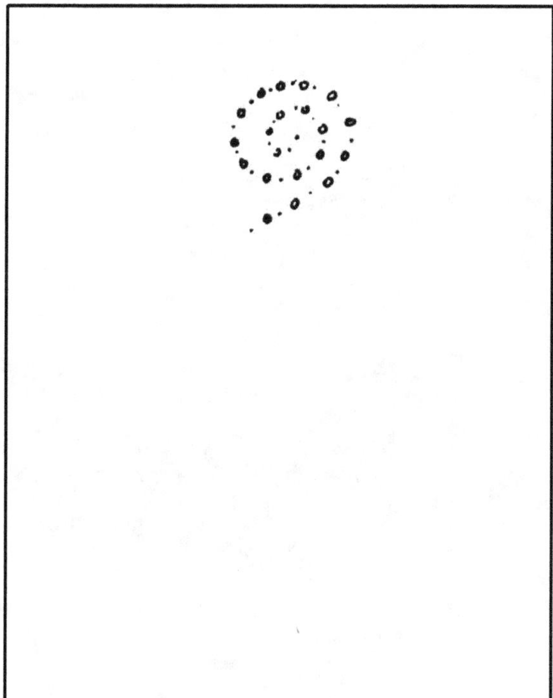

4.1

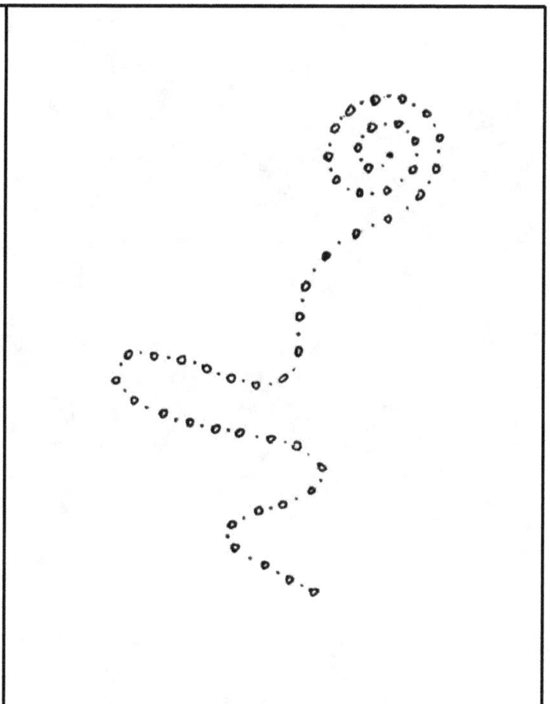

4.2

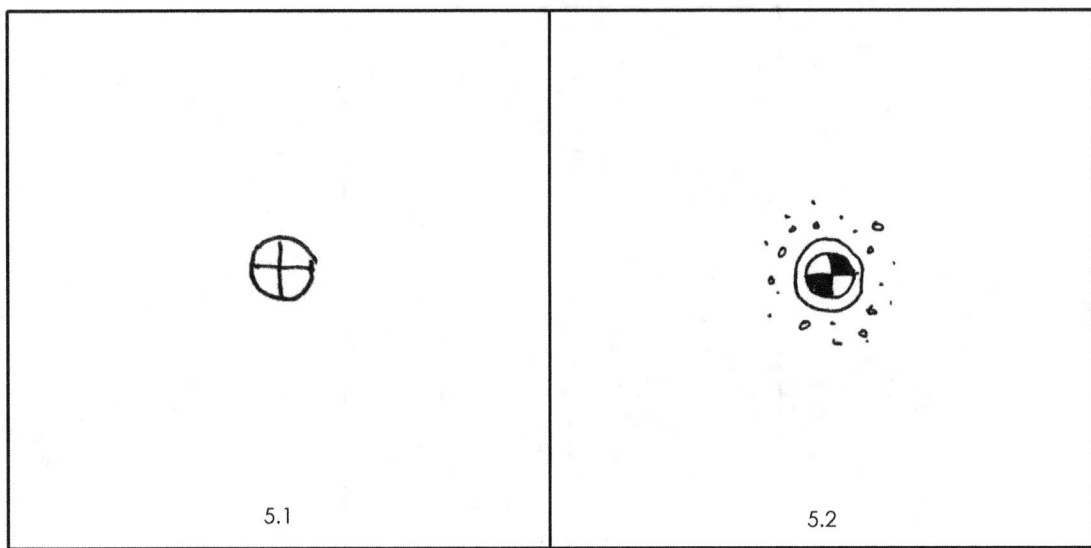

5.1   5.2

Create Abstracts
with NADIA RUSS

T he following pages (35-45) invite you to draw abstracts with Nadia Russ here

and now. All you need is the thin ink pen because thick pen will leave marks on another side of the page. Complete sections of the following abstracts with the offered repetitive patterns.

When you focus on repetitive patterns' drawing, in a few minutes, you feel your breath as it enters and leaves your nostrils. You enter the meditative state of mind. Meditation is a positive brain-changing activity that increases your brain functions. It helps people suffering from depression, anxiety, post-traumatic stress disorder. There's strong connection between meditation, healthier immune system and happiness. Meditation process increases your learning abilities and memory. Through meditation you achieve sublime state of mind.

The repetitive patterns' drawing process is creative process. It is fun and helps you develop your artistic skills and intuition. You will learn how to create the balanced and interesting compositions.

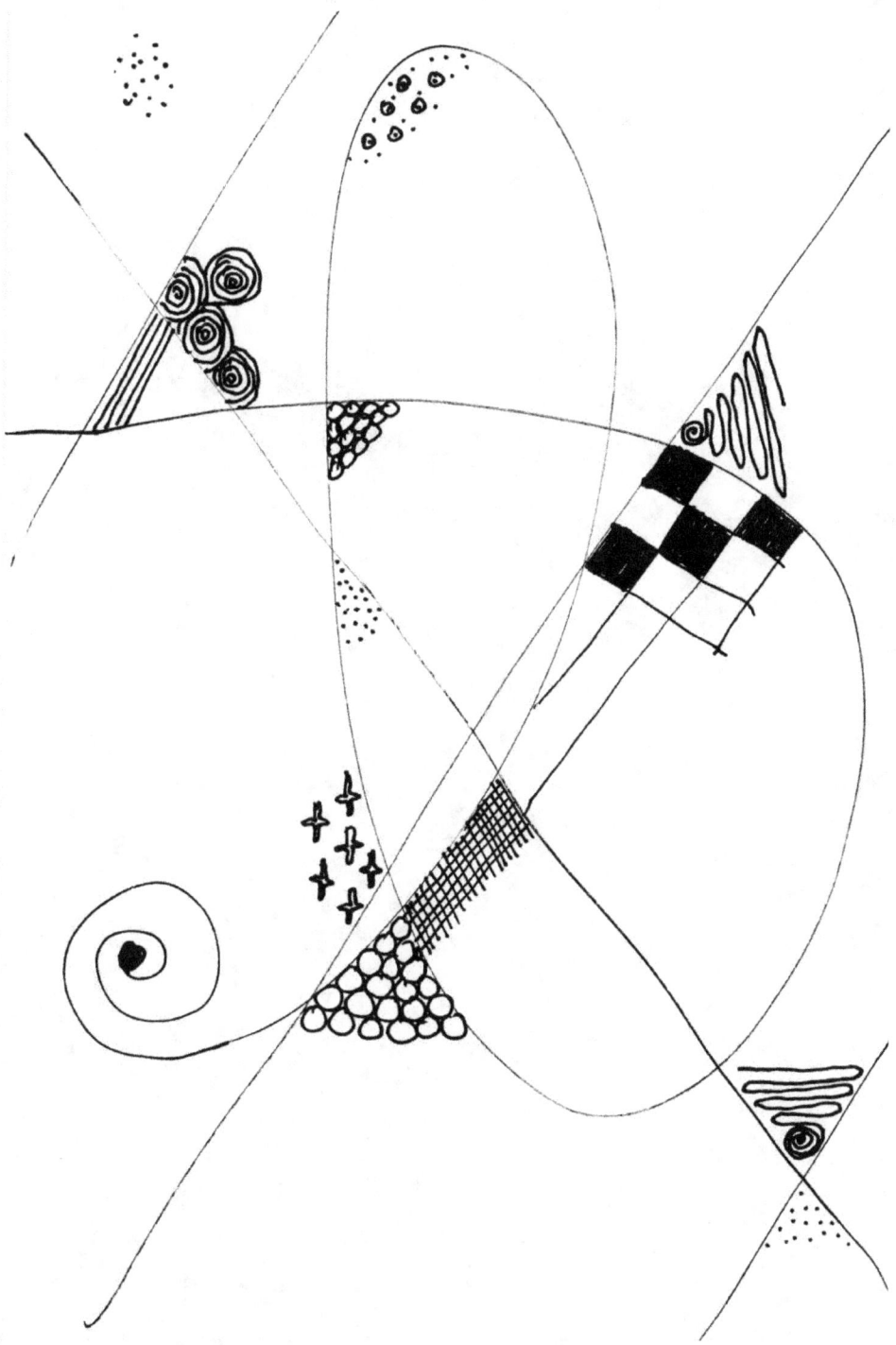

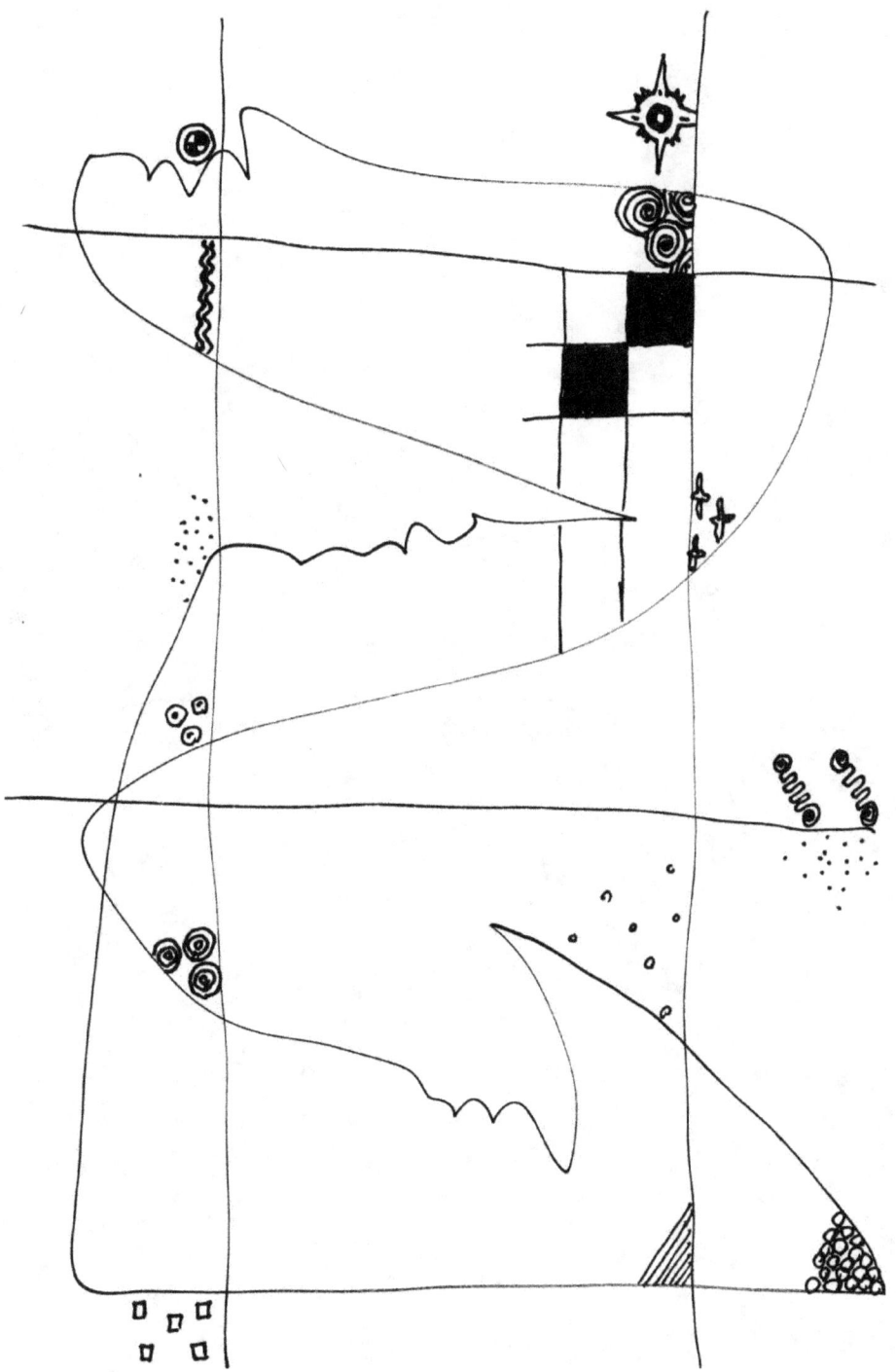

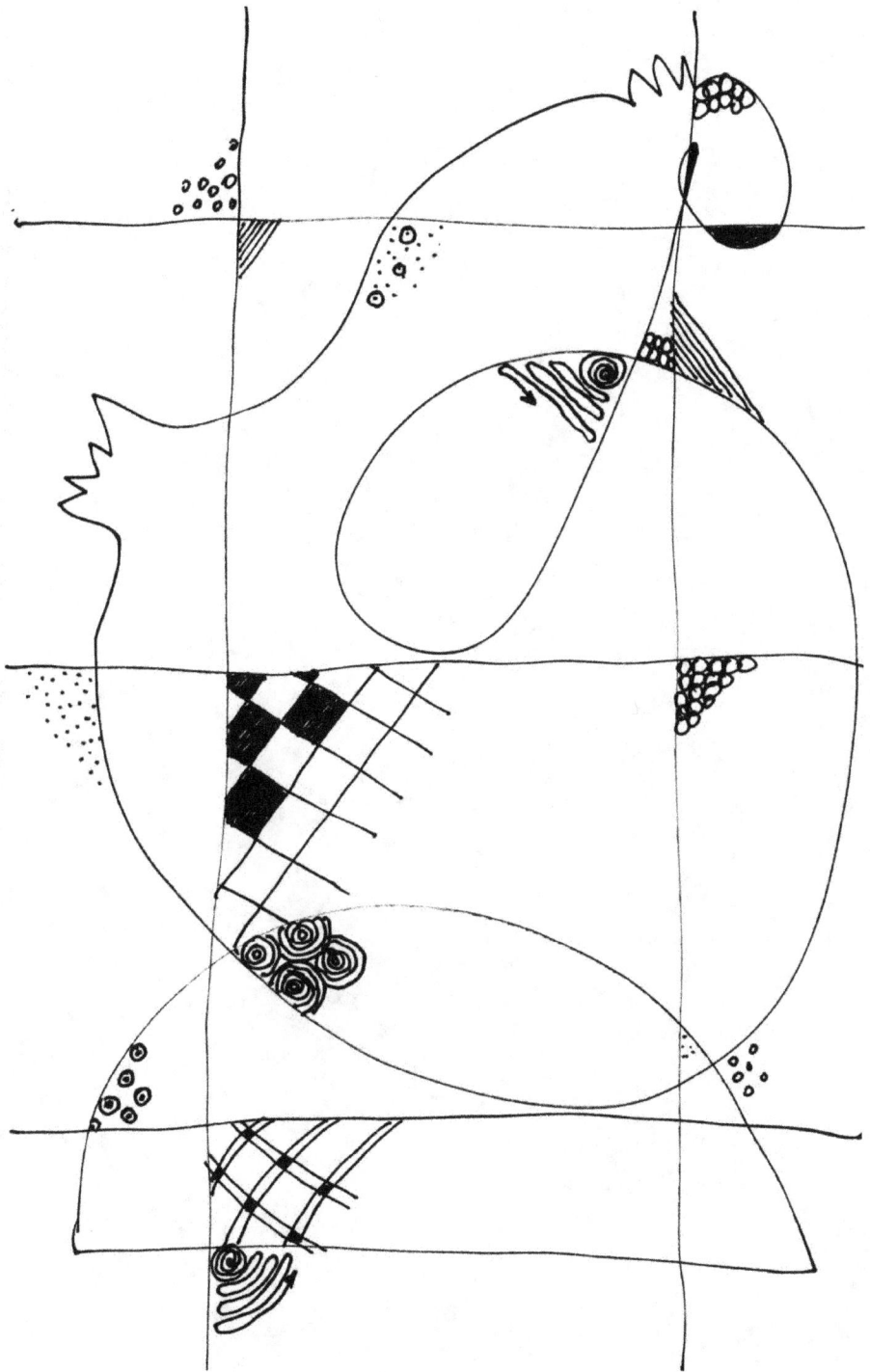

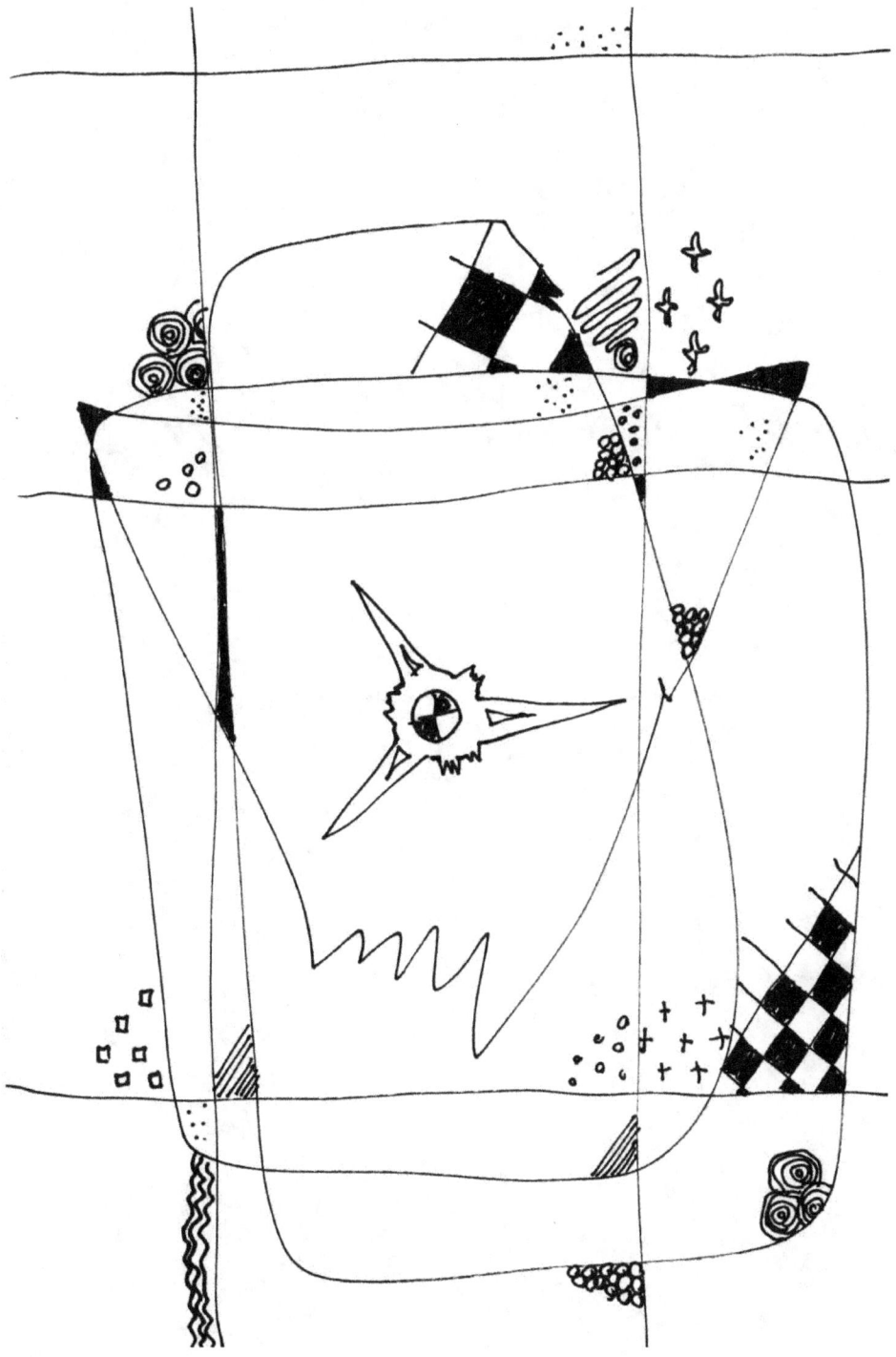

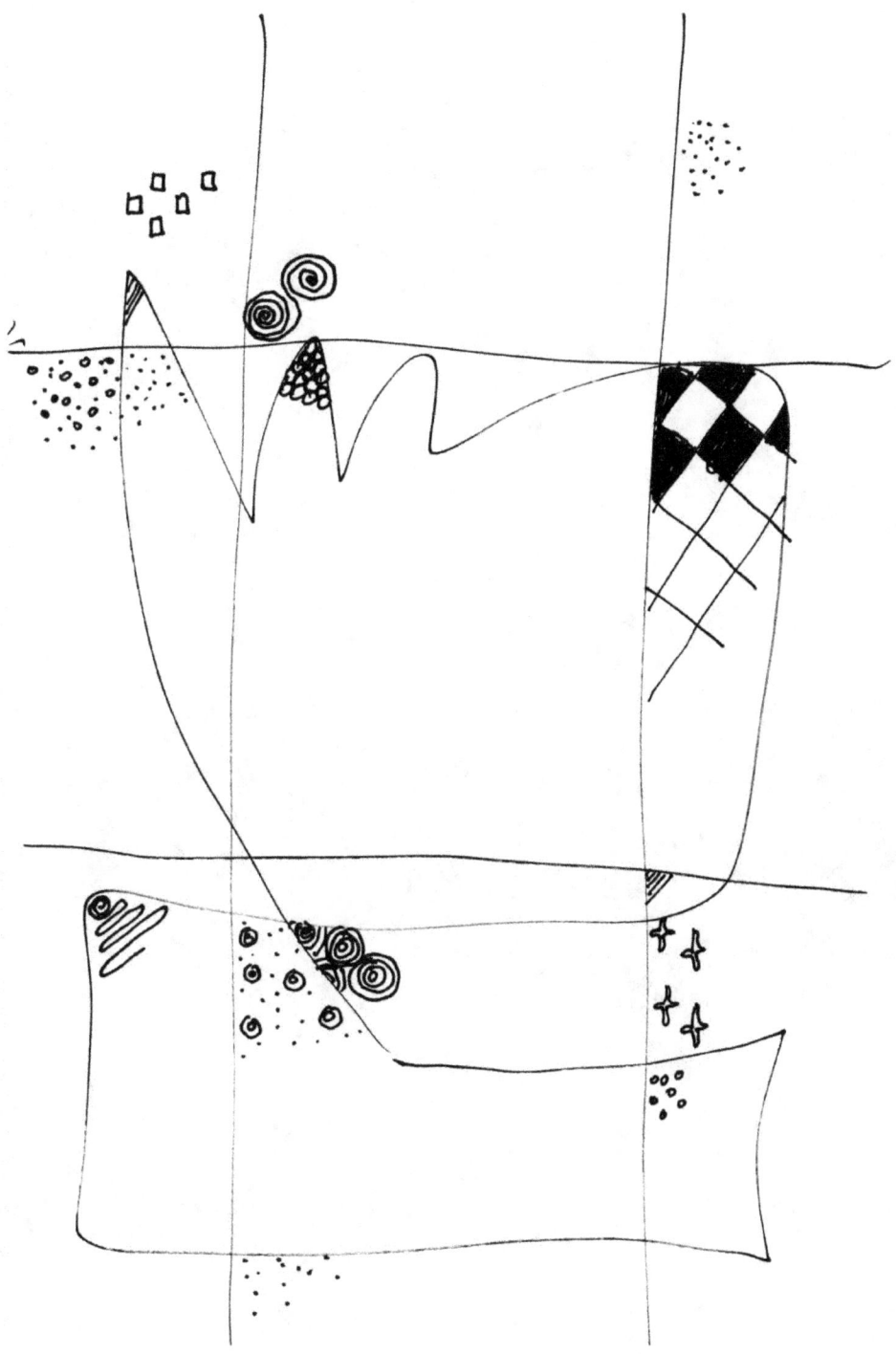

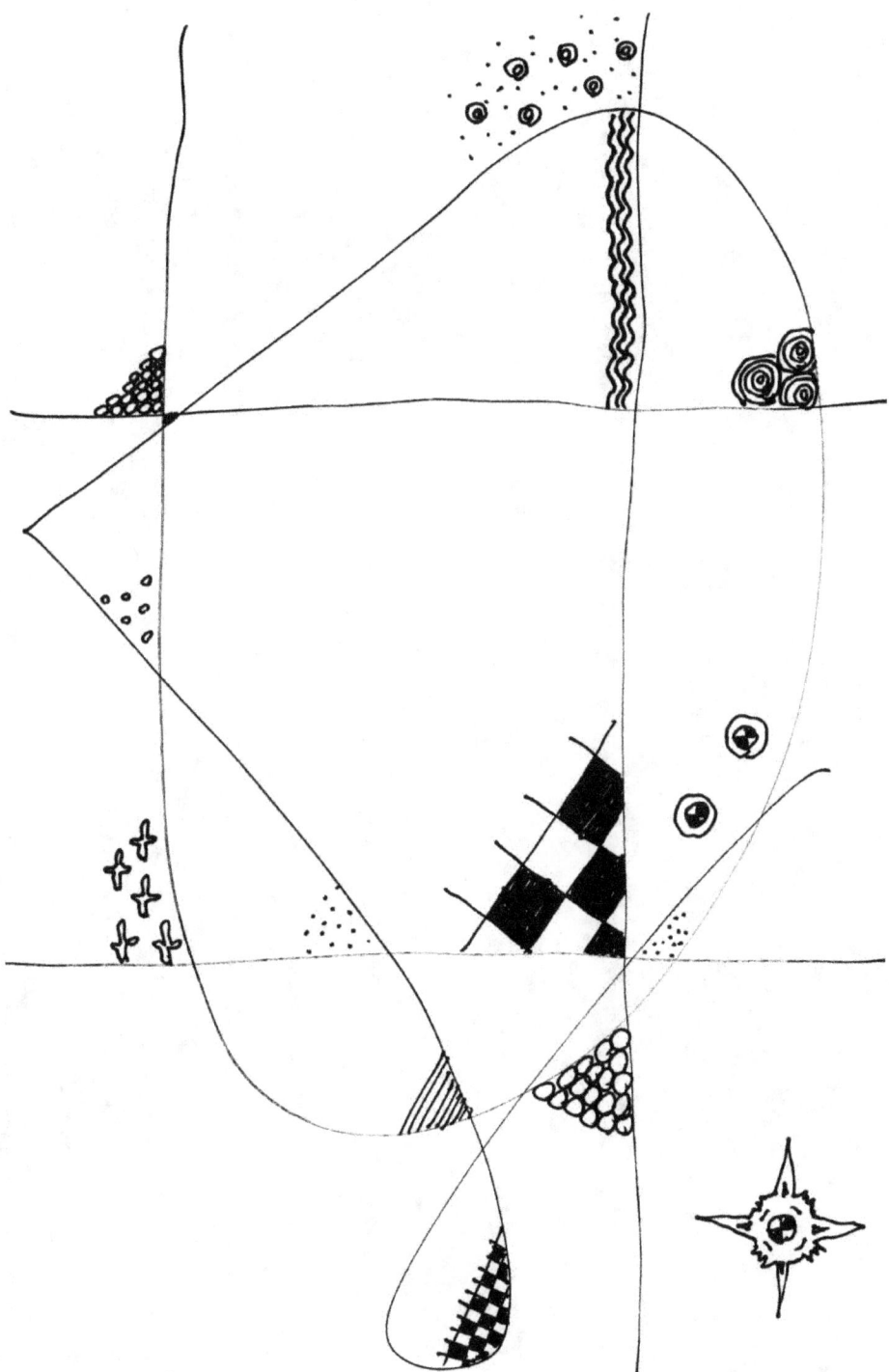

In the following pages (47, 49, 51, and 53) fill sections with different repetitive patterns, some sections leave blank. This is intuitive drawing, focus on details, create, use your imagination, and meditate. You will enjoy the process or will suffer. It is natural feelings, they depend on your skills. Feeling of enjoyment comes with professionalism.

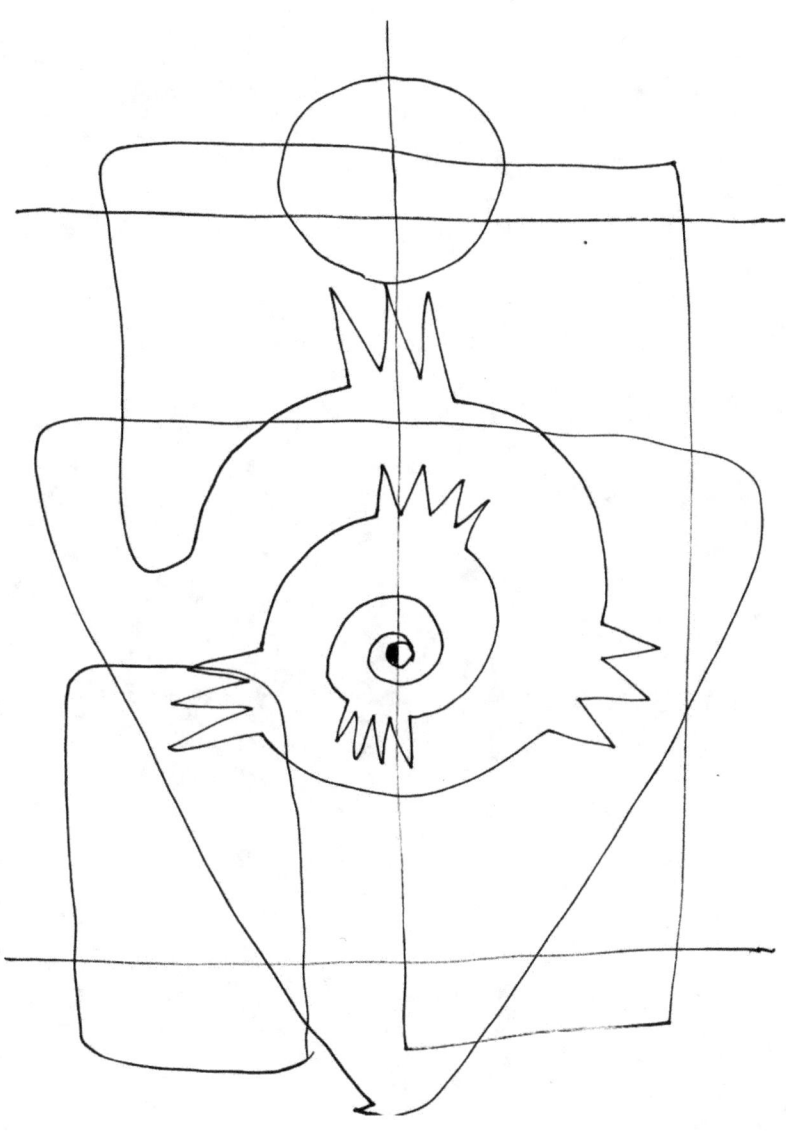

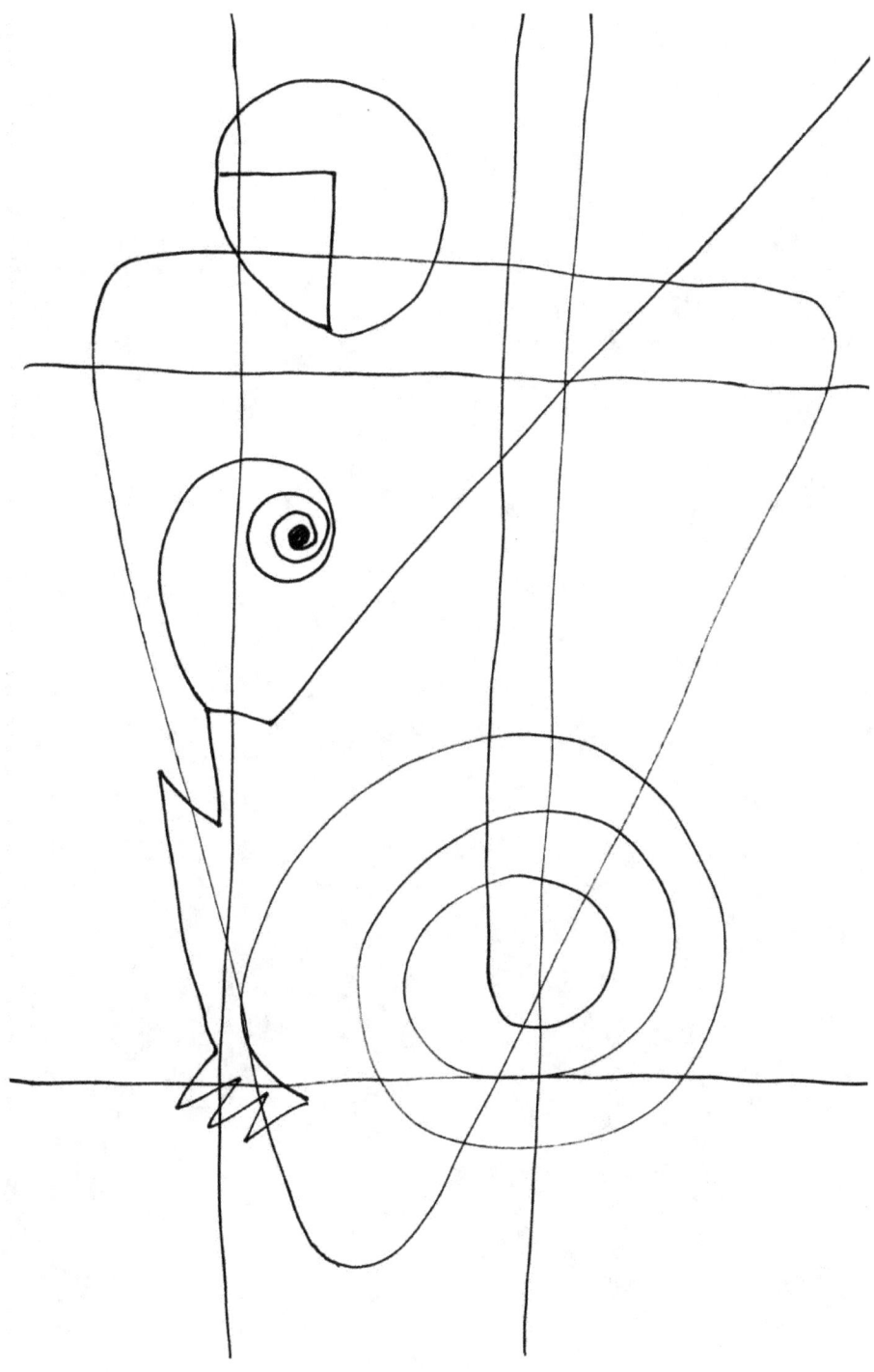

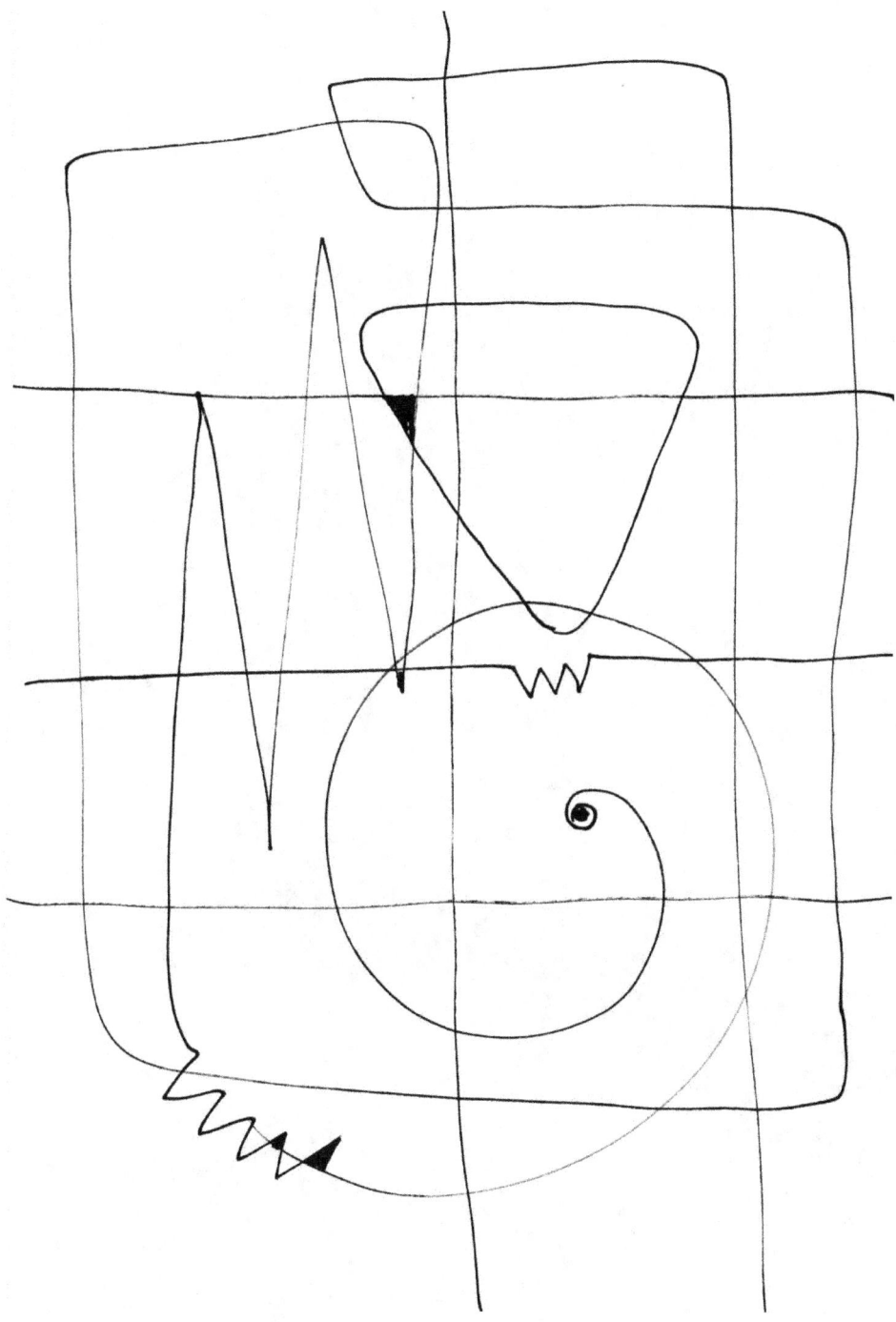

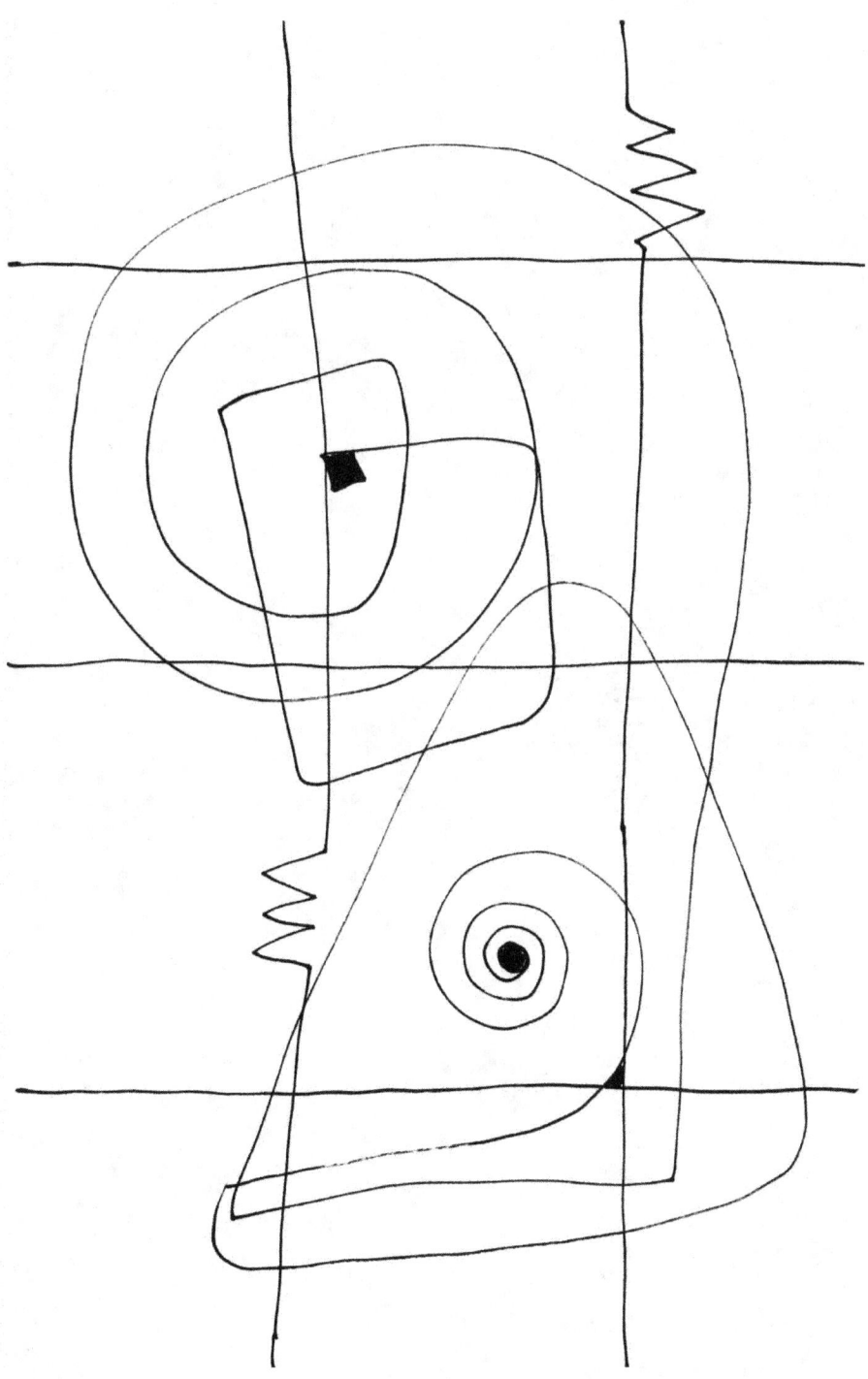

Create your repetitive
patterns Gallery

The following pages invite you to create your personal repetitive patterns' Gallery here and now. All you need is thin ink pen. Fill each section with different repetitive pattern. Use your imagination, make different combinations and variations of the line, circles, squares, dots, triangles, ovals; twist and turn your line, follow your creative instinct. This process will help you develop your artistic skills and imagination. You will need these patterns' Gallery later, when you will draw your future images.

1	2	3
4	5	6

7	8	9
10	11	12
13	14	15
16	17	18

19	20	21
22	23	24
25	26	27
28	29	30

31	32	33
34	35	36
37	38	39
40	41	42

43	44	45
46	47	48
49	50	51
52	53	54

Create your abstract drawings from the scratch

The following pages (65-72) are for you to create your NeoPopRealism abstracts-drawings from the scratch. A few abstracts (pages 60-64) are here to give you some ideas about the variations. You should not copy them; create new, different abstracts. Always use ink pen. Do not worry if you make a mistake or two. Do not try to erase them; they will disappear with new repetitive patterns that will balance the whole composition. Draw focusing on each detail. Open your mind to possibilities and remember that impossible is nothing.

Draw your images with ease. The repetitive patterns' drawing process will open you doors to the level of meditation and relaxation you never experienced before. Eventually, you will discover new you, with wide eyes open to new opportunities in art and life.

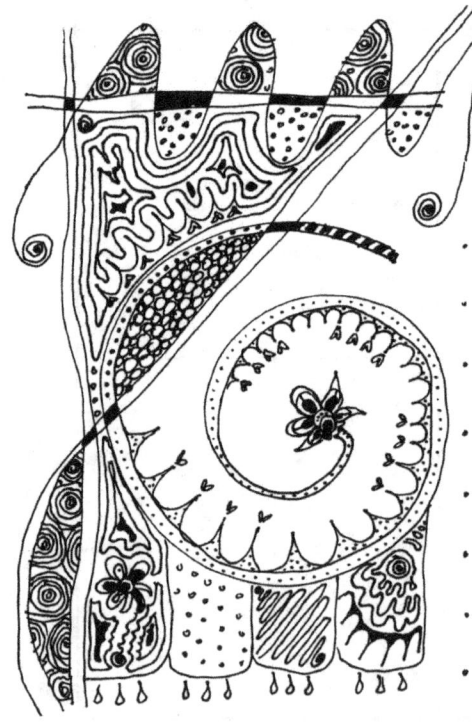

Nadia Russ, Abstract 5, *Meditation 8*, ink on paper

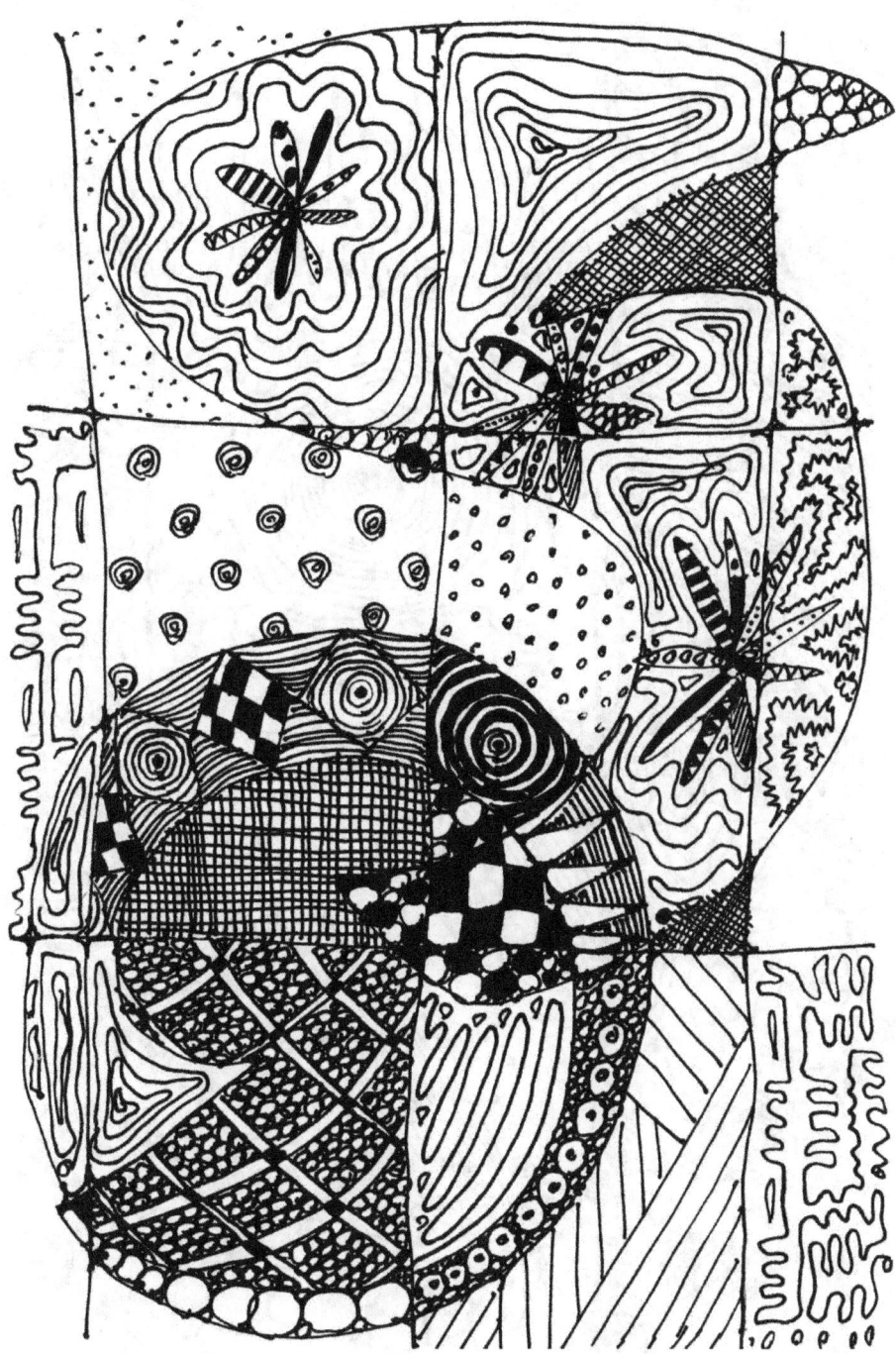

Nadia Russ, Abstract 6, *Meditation 7*, ink on paper

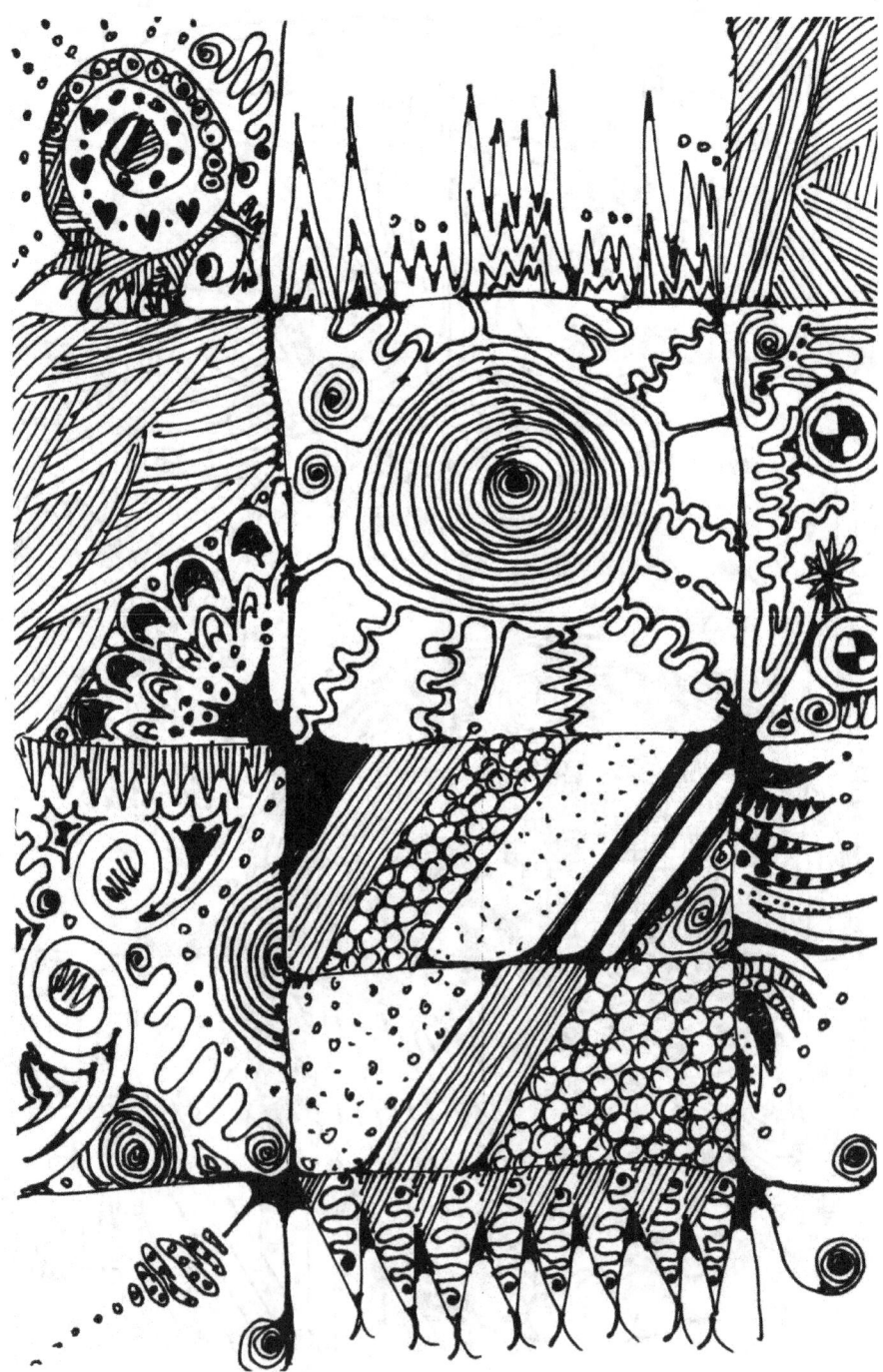

Nadia Russ, Abstract 7, *Meditation 6*, ink on paper

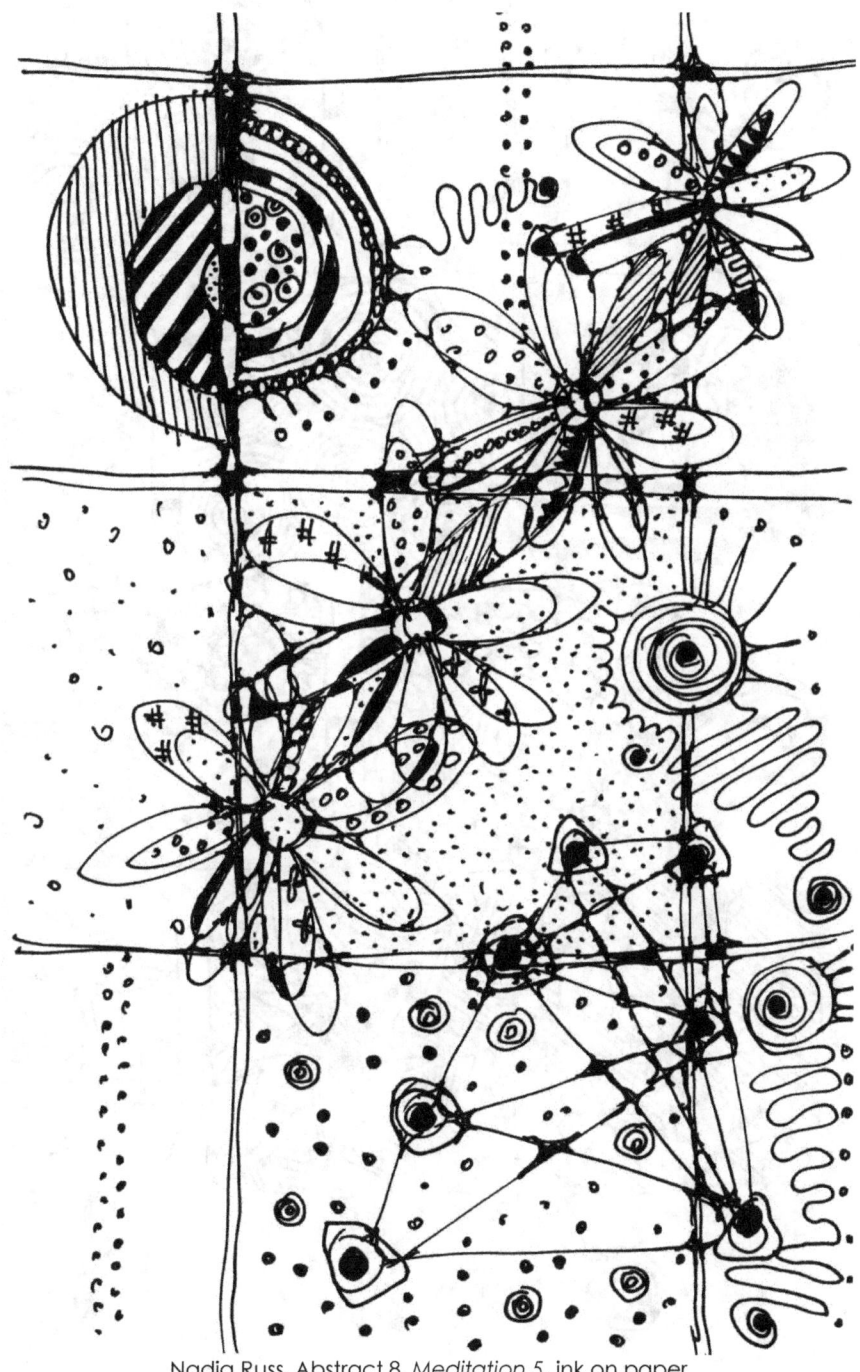

Nadia Russ, Abstract 8, *Meditation 5,* ink on paper

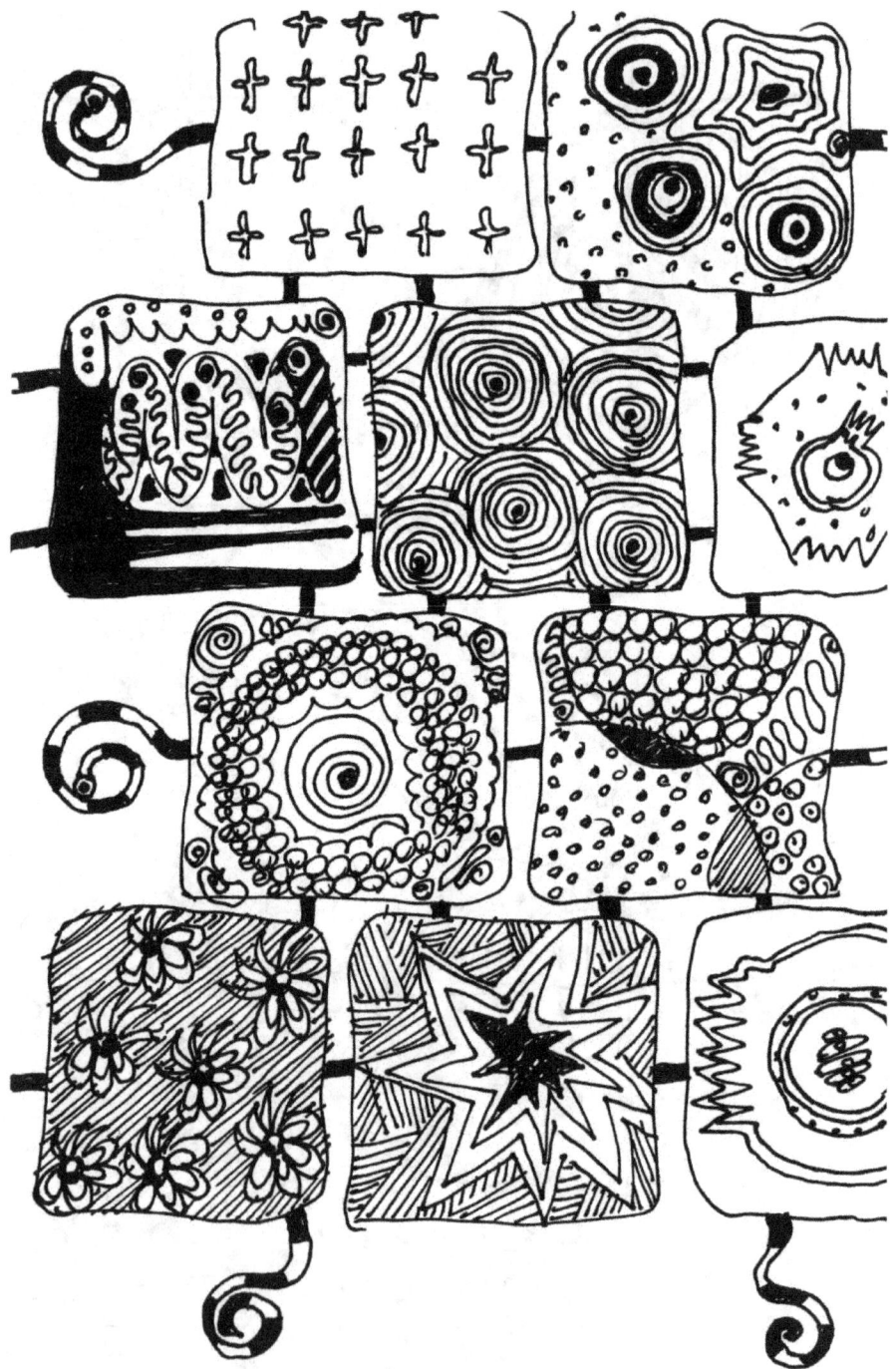

Nadia Russ, Abstract 9, *Meditation 4*, ink on paper

About NeoPopRealism creator NADIA RUSS

Nadia Russ (aka Nadejda Maloletneva) was born into a former professional military officer's family. As a child, she began studying art from famous masters of the past through art books and reproductions, which her mother Vera was collecting in their home. Nadia daily heard about and saw the reproductions of works of Leonardo da Vinci, Michelangelo, Rafael, contemporary Russian artists such as Petrov-Vodkin.

She began painting and drawing seriously in 1989. A few months later, her first ink drawings were exhibited in a group exhibition in famous Moscow's Manege and later, in other Moscow's art galleries. In 1992, she successfully showed her work in New York City.

In 1996-2000, Nadia resided in the Bahamas, where her work gained some special brightness. There, she got her pseudonym to her original 'Nadejda Maloletneva', which was easier to pronounce - 'Nadia Russ'. In 2000-2001, in Xanadu hotel, she operated her Art Gallery Club 13.

In 2000, she moved to the United States, where she lives up until present. January 4, 2003, Nadia Russ created a word NeoPopRealism and manifested internationally new style of visual arts which combines the brightness and simplicity of Pop Art with deep and psychological realism and has graphic nature. Her artworks are in private and permanent public collections including MOYA - Museum of Young Art in Vienna (Austria), Simferopol and Sumy Art Museums in Ukraine, Kinsey Institute of Indiana University (USA), Ukrainian Museum in New York City (USA), WEAM - World Erotic Art Museum in Miami (USA), Schacknow Museum of Fine Arts (USA), Historical Museum of Fort Lauderdale (USA), Lebedyn and Konotop Art Museums (Ukraine), D. Burliuk Foundation (Ukraine), and other.

In 2008-2010, Nadia Russ founded and juried Int'l NeoPopRealism Starz Art competitions. She authored a few art-related books such as "NeoPopRealism Starz: 21st Century ART" two volumes, "New Millennium ART", "Fort Lauderdale 100: A Must-Have Collector's Edition." She is the founder (2007) of the *NeoPopRealism Journal & Wonderpedia*, publications online, dedicated to arts, culture, books, news, celebrities and more. Nadia Russ lives in New York City and Florida. Visit her website at www.nadiaruss.com.

Conclusion

"**W**hat is Art?"

Now, when you have learned how to draw the NeoPopRealism abstract images, you might have your answer to this open question. We'll be happy to hear from you, e-mail us to NeopoprealismPress@mail.com. If you have a blog, post there images of your NeoPopRealismt ink drawings and a story about how you learned to draw them. Have a wonderful journey to the world of NeoPopRealism!

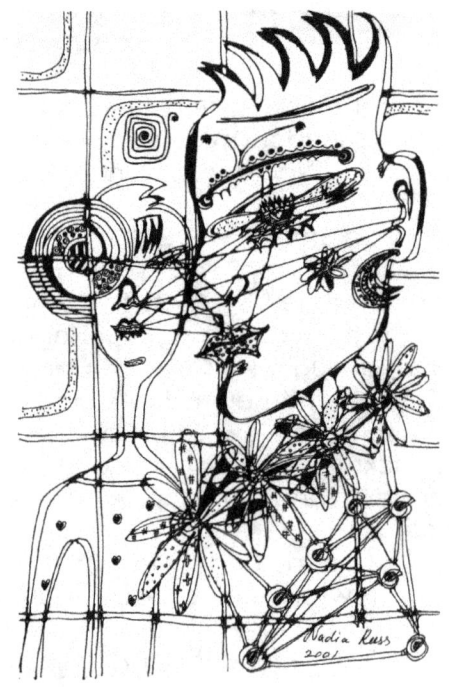

Nadia Russ, *People*, 6.5"x11", ink on paper, 2001

NeoPopRealism ten canons for happier life

1. Be beautiful.
2. Be creative and productive; never stop studying and learning.
3. Be peace-loving, positive-minded.
4. Do not accept communist philosophy.
5. Be free-minded, do the best you can to move the world to peace and harmony.
6. Be family oriented, self-disciplined.
7. Be free spirited. Follow your dreams, if they are not destructive, but constructive.
8. Believe in god. God is one.
9. Be supportive to those who need you, be generous.
10. Create your life as a great adventurous story.

Created by Nadia Russ in 2004

Additional books - teaching / learning material on NeoPopRealism Ink and pen drawing for adults, teenagers and children.

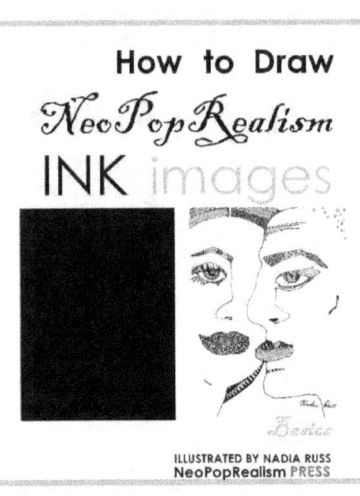

ISBN: 9780615515755
FOR TEENS & ADULTS

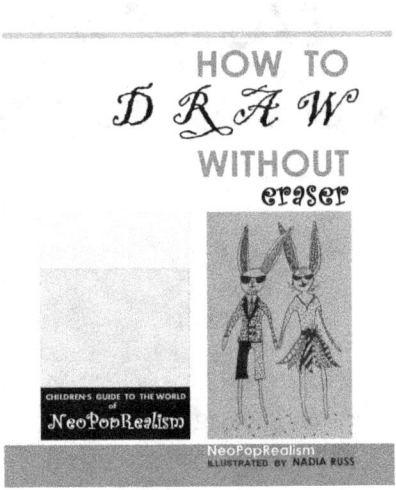

ISBN: 9780615521824
FOR CHILDREN

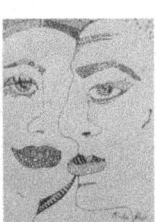

Book "*How to Draw NeoPopRealism Ink Images: Basics*" in Russian translation.
ISBN: 9780615516967

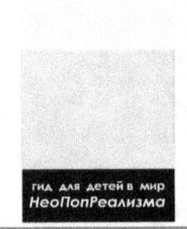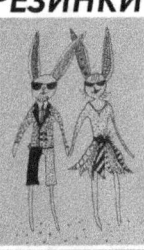

Book "*How to Draw Without Eraser: Backgrounds*" in Russian translation.
ISBN: 9780615523484

www.ingramcontent.com/pod-product-compliance
Lightning Source LLC
Chambersburg PA
CBHW081119180526
45170CB00008B/2915